A CONCISE HISTORY OF CANADA

A CONCISE HISTORY OF

CANADA

GERALD S. GRAHAM

with 181 illustrations

A STUDIO BOOK

THE VIKING PRESS · NEW YORK

Frontispiece:
The Newfoundland cod fisheries initiated Europe's enduring connection with Canada.

Contents

To Laura, James and Constance

Preface

To attempt to invoke the realities of Canadian history within thirty thousand words is a hazardous undertaking. If the national pattern were clear-cut the process of condensation would be relatively simple; but the Canada which emerges as a federation after 1867 is a compound of disparate elements which have, in their original shape and being, little relationship with each other. Despite the suggestive trails blazed by the westward retreating beaver (whose importance in earlier international relations equalled that of the cod), there is no wholly satisfying 'frontier thesis' to mark the processes of national growth. Before the union the isolated colonies on the Atlantic and Pacific coasts of the continent lived completely different lives. For more than two and a half centuries after John Cabot made his disputed landfall, Newfoundland remained 'a great English ship moored near the Banks'. United before 1791 and forced together again in 1840, the two peoples of the St Lawrence Valley never ceased to pursue their separate ways, and to cherish their separate languages, separate histories and separate ambitions. Consequently, when the loose scaffolding of federal authority was thrust upon the provinces of British North America, the builders' work had to be accomplished in defiance of both history and geography.

History presents probably the more serious obstacle because, until the end of the eighteenth century, Canada's fortunes were deeply entwined

◀ The Cabot Trail.

with the rivalries of two European powers, France and Britain, and, after 1783, with an imposing neighbour, the United States. In the nineteenth century, the development of Canadian national autonomy – the achievement of responsible government and Dominion status – cannot be separated from the evolution of British colonial policy, any more than the struggle for national identity can be separated from the pattern of American industrialization. The risk of blurring the picture of an emerging nation is, therefore, considerable; any handy chronology of progress is apt to be lost amid distracting generalizations on external influence and background. Moreover, in building upwards from early foundations, while the risk of distorting the past to gratify the present may be trivial, there is always the danger of striving for some underlying concept of unity that may not exist. In a compressed piece of reconstruction such as this, it is tempting to streamline national development in the interests of simplicity and clarity.

But unifying threads are hard to come by, even in the geographical setting, and this the weary traveller may appreciate as his train twists and charges from Halifax to Vancouver, through the maze of religion and race, pastoral countryside and sombre wasteland, rock and prairie, mountain and forest. For the greater part of the journey, his road follows a narrow corridor which is the habitable area of Canada. Outside it, to the south, lies the United States, never more than two hundred miles away; northward, the impinging mass of the great Laurentian Shield slopes ponderously towards Hudson Bay and the Arctic Sea. Road and rail symbolize the pertinacious efforts of Canadians to achieve some sort of physical unity. Yet, despite the ties of cement and steel, the forces that operate on the nation state still tend to be centrifugal: the Maritime provinces look south as well as west; British Columbia, isolated behind her mountain barriers, looks south as well as east, while Quebec continues to gaze inwards, sombrely contemplating two centuries of existence as a subject race. The search for a national identity has been frustrating for the historian as for the politician, but a story of unending effort is by no means colourless, nor the net result inglorious. Although it may never possess the cultural homogeneity of Australia or even the United States, the Canadian nation has at least survived, and in a world of savage tribal disorder, it remains, by comparison, a considerable experiment in toleration and compromise.

In recent years, research in Canadian history has developed enor- mously in range and quality, and this brief interpretation could not have been undertaken without the guidance provided by that highly profes- sional quarterly, the *Canadian Historical Review*. My debt to its contri- butors, whose own scholarly works have revolutionized the subject in the last forty years, is beyond reckoning.

Gerald S. Graham
King's College
University of London
January 1967

Secundùm littora Novæ Franciæ multæ in sicup... ... Balenæ,

Chapter One

The name *Canada* is an Indian word which in the sixteenth century described the first French settlements along the north shore of the St Lawrence River between the Ottawa and the Saguenay rivers. Following the British conquest it included for a few years the vast triangle between the rivers Mississippi and Ohio, now the American states of Wisconsin, Michigan, Indiana, Illinois and Ohio, and between 1841 and 1867, comprised the present provinces of Ontario and Quebec. A 'dominion from sea to sea' – a territory almost as large as the whole of Europe – began to take shape as a nation only when the Atlantic provinces of Nova Scotia, New Brunswick and Prince Edward Island – roughly the old French Acadia – combined with Canada and with British Columbia to produce, between 1867 and 1873, a federal union which cynics with some justice described as little more than 'a geographical expression'.

Today the name *Canada* is applied to more than half the continent and islands of North America, an area estimated to include some one and a half million square miles. But apart from the industrial salient between the St Lawrence River and the Great Lakes (which contains nearly two-thirds of the population) settlement is contained in an uneven ribbon some three hundred miles in breadth, stretching almost five thousand miles from St John's, Newfoundland to Vancouver Island. The rest of the country is virtually uninhabited, and, even with the aid of the aeroplane, not yet fully explored.

◀ *Nova Francia*. Detail of a map by Petrus Plancius, 1592.

In the east lies the fog-swept island of Newfoundland, one of the oldest settlements in North America, and since 1949 the tenth province of Canada. As centre of the North Atlantic fisheries it had been for centuries an object of international rivalry. Today, the shallow waters of the Grand Banks, cooled by the Labrador current, still provide feeding-grounds for the fastidious and prolific cod, which remains a basic staple of the Newfoundland economy. Recent years, however, have seen the development of a pulp and paper industry and the discovery in both Labrador and Newfoundland of rich mineral deposits, especially iron.

Across the Cabot Strait, Nova Scotia, narrowly attached to the hinterland of New Brunswick, juts into the Atlantic, its northern arm shielding the garden of Prince Edward Island. Geographically, these Maritime provinces are more nearly linked with New England than with central Canada, and this isolation from the industrial heartland, com-bined with the strong economic and social attachments to the United States, helps to explain the slow growth of population. Even after the building of the railways, remoteness from the thriving cities in the St Lawrence Valley continued to foster a strong regional loyalty which, to the visitor from Toronto or Montreal, seemed at times to approximate separate nationality. Although both Nova Scotia and New Brunswick have rich agricultural pockets, the mainland is largely covered with forest, offering moose and deer to the avid hunter as well as providing the raw materials for lumber and pulp mills which remain the backbone of the economy. As in Newfoundland, both inshore and deep-sea fisheries employ a large proportion of the coastal population, and over the past half-century iron and steel production has developed spasmodically, based on Cape Breton's coal resources and the high-grade iron ores of Newfoundland and Labrador.

Valley of the St Lawrence Montreal and Toronto, homes of the most important commercial enterprises and big corporations, symbolize the wealth and bustling business ways of a region that contains almost two-thirds of the people of Canada and nearly eighty per cent of the country's industries. But history has unhappily split this great Valley of the St Lawrence, and the frictions between French-speaking and English-speaking Canadians have some-times threatened to immobilize government and shatter the federal union.

Newfoundland fishing village, Hibb's Cove, Conception Bay.

A coal mine in Cape Breton.

Timber from the New Brunswick forests is transported down the Restigouche River, famous for its salmon.

The centres of Canadian commerce and finance are Montreal (*left*) and Toronto (*right*), both modern cities with busy ports.

For over three hundred years the province of Quebec maintained an almost exclusively French and Catholic culture, and the determination of the inhabitants to survive as a distinct cultural enclave on a continent chiefly English-speaking and Protestant has led to bitter struggles against both real and imagined attempts at assimilation. French Canadians look with distrust on the acquisitive and accomplished business breed across the Ottawa River, and they have remained suspicious of what they call 'English imperialism' – sufficiently to resist with passion the imposition of national conscription in two world wars.

The secluded village of Tadoussac (*above*) in French Quebec provides a contrast with one of the world's busiest thoroughfares: Sault Ste Marie, Ontario (*below*).

In contrast to the seclusion of Quebec, Ontario belongs to the world and to North America. Created at the outset by United Empire Loyalists and post-Loyalists who migrated after the American Revolution, its population before the Second World War was three-quarters British in origin. In recent years, however, as a result of constant European immigration, the province has become far more cosmopolitan, and in atmosphere, manners and business methods, more American. Whether the newcomer travels the north or the south shore of the St Lawrence Seaway, he may feel that one lake port looks much like another.

Above Lake Superior, a painting by Lawren Harris.

The Laurentian Shield Dividing eastern and western Canada like a ravaged no-man's-land stretches the Laurentian Shield. Covering nearly half of the country's land surface, this awesome mass of pre-Cambrian rock embraces Hudson Bay, encroaching on both Labrador and the North-West Territories, and descending southward below Lake Superior. On this glacier-scoured terrain of scrub, swamp and twisted rock, agriculture could never take more than feeble root, and many years were to elapse before Canadians were to find within the fractured strata some three-quarters of their mineral wealth. Unfortunately, except on its westward fringes in Alberta, the Shield contains no coal, but the ice which once gouged its tormented surface left a second heritage – a vast network of lakes and rivers offering immeasurable resources of water power.

20

Photographer's impression of clouds over the waters of Lake Superior. ▶

The industrial West.

On the plains of Saskatchewan (*above*) is the enormous potash mill of the International Mineral and Chemical Corporation at Esterhazy. Forest surrounds the Imperial Oil drilling rig (*right*) in the Rainbow-Zama Lake area of north-western Alberta, the centre of Canada's oil exploration.

But the Shield remains a harsh and forbidding barrier, creating by its stubborn immensity problems both political and financial that persist up to the present time. How, for example, can bulk materials be moved economically over vacant stretches as long as two thousand miles? How can one profitably transport Saskatchewan's potash or Alberta's oil across Manitoba and north-western Ontario to the industrial markets of the east against the competition of spur lines that divert traffic to the nearby United States? Understandably engineers and scientists are giving increasing attention to means of bridging the Empty Quarter by pipelines. But such methods of circumvention will not mean conquest. Freight trains will still forge through the resentful wastes – the homeland of the trapper, the prospector and the painter, a lonely land that is transformed for a moment each year by the blazing illuminations of autumn leaves reflected in ten thousand lakes.

The new town of Thompson in northern Manitoba. Smoke rises from the plant of the International Nickel Company.

The West   The burgeoning prairies consisting of Manitoba, Saskatchewan and
Alberta stretch westward for some eight hundred miles to the foothills of
the Rocky Mountains. Before the Second World War these were essen‐
tially wheatlands, and over fifty per cent of the employable men were
engaged in agriculture. But time has modified the once bitter conflict of

Grain elevators in the Saskatchewan prairies.

interest between the grain grower and the eastern industrialist. Manitoba with its Winnipeg gateway to the West, and its mines, railway shops and factories, Saskatchewan rich in potash and oil, and Alberta even richer in oil and gas, have given the West a flourishing stake in secondary industry. Yet differences of interest and outlook still exist between the

25

LET THE BIG CHIEF BEWARE!

A protest from Manitoba against the carrying monopoly given to the Canadian Pacific Railway by 'big chief' John A. Macdonald; cartoon of 1886.

The Winnipeg General Strike of 1919.

industrial capitalism of the St Lawrence Valley and the prevailing agrarianism of the prairies, an antithesis which is regularly expressed in federal elections. Out of the West in 1920 came a third political party, the Progressives, based on the farmers' co-operative movement, and the precursor of a national farmer-labour party, the neo-socialist Cooperative Commonwealth Federation, founded in Regina in 1933. At almost the same time, Alberta produced an evangelical high-school principal and lay-preacher, William Aberhart, whose successful Social Credit movement was to dispute the means of salvation, both spiritual and economic, with the CCF, and ultimately to ensure political control of the province.

Admittedly the rise of left-wing unorthodoxy to combat the two old parties of respectable 'big business' was chiefly a consequence of the great depression. Public suffering inevitably led to discontent with conven-

THE SCRIP THAT DIDN'T COME HOME

Cartoon of William Aberhart, apostle of Social Credit.

tional instruments of government. Yet the search for alternatives was facilitated not only by dire poverty, but by the independent character of the new, politically unattached population. The West has been a melting-pot of many races, and while the immigrants gradually assimilated the ways and manners of British North America, they never entirely lost their cultural roots that reached far back to the Vistula and the Dnieper, the Thames and the Seine.

The North-West Territories lie north of the sixtieth parallel between the Yukon Territory and Hudson Bay and include the islands of the Arctic Archipelago. This vast area administered from Ottawa is broken into three divisions – Mackenzie on the west, Keewatin bordering Hudson Bay, and Franklin, which includes nearly all the islands of the Arctic Archipelago.

The North-West Territories

The original inhabitants of Canada were Indians and Eskimos. *Above*, Indians of the Sarcee ('Not Good') tribe, who live along the eastern border of the Rocky Mountains.

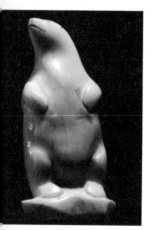

Eskimo carving of soap-stone.

28

For more than three hundred years after Martin Frobisher's first voyage to Baffin Island, explorers tried, during the short summer season, to penetrate this northern mosaic in search of a North-West Passage. The native peoples whom they encountered in the course of their travels were not generally aggressive or warlike; yet the impact of European culture was in the long run more deadly in its effects than any clash of arms. By the beginning of the twentieth century, the Eskimos and Indians of the far north seemed doomed to extinction. At the last moment, they were spared this fate, the remnants surviving as objects of anthropological interest and makers of curios and soap-stone polar bears. Even today their numbers are limited in comparison with the white population, who have been drawn to the North-West Territories by mining opportunities and government development programmes. Out of a total of 23,000 in 1961, 42 per cent were Europeans, 35 per cent Eskimo, and 23 per cent Indian.

The modern Eskimo, collecting snow for water. ▶

First issue of a
Klondike newspaper
published in 1898
during the gold-rush.

It is perhaps understandable that the scene of the last great gold-rush should have become even more completely white man's country. Sixty-five years after the famous Klondike strike in 1896, the population of the Yukon Territory was 14,500 souls; of these, 85 per cent were of European stock, and slightly over 14 per cent were Indian. Forty Eskimos contributed a percentage of 0·03.

Throughout the Northland, gold has been the mainstay of the invader, with agriculture, forestry and electric power as its handmaidens. The fur trade too has become subsidiary to the mining industry; sealskins and white fox, beaver, marten, mink and lynx are still traded for provisions, traps, guns and other equipment. Probably for centuries the caribou had been the main food staple, especially of the Chipewyan Indians, but migrating herds of ten thousand and more no longer move across the Keewatin tundra to melt into the infinity of the Barren Lands. The repeating rifle in the hands of both white man and native has reduced the estimated four million head of sixty years ago to about a tenth of that number. Yet there has been little of the wanton killing such as brought

Migrating caribou
in the North-West
Territories.

30

Gold prospectors climbing the Chilkoot Pass, Alaska, 1898–9.

the buffalo to the verge of extinction a century ago. Increased consump⁄tion in the interest of the fur trade has been chiefly responsible for upsetting a primitive balance, and thus threatening caribou as well as native survival. In Canada the record of the 'nearly⁄vanished' is a formidable one, and there is no easy solution for technically triumphant man, trapped by the instruments of his own achievement.

British Columbia   Bordering on the Pacific Ocean, British Columbia is a region of high plateaus, deep canyons and fast⁄running rivers. Inevitably the physical and mental isolation produced by nature's barriers fosters a strong local sentiment. Ottawa seems very far away; as with the Maritime provinces, the easiest approaches lie southward to the United States. There are several distinct mountain ranges running roughly parallel in a north⁄west direction, but the most important barrier is the eastern Rockies, a con⁄tinuous range averaging about fifty miles in width and rising to more than 12,000 feet at the highest points.

The buffalo, once extensively hunted for meat and sport, has been saved from total extinction by law.

A forest ranger in ▶ the eastern Rockies near the Continental Divide.

Western British Columbia is dominated by the Coast mountains, a massive range nearly 125 miles broad in the south, whose submerged flank provides the deeply indented coastline of bays and fiords, as well as a coastal archipelago that includes Vancouver Island. The climate, which is determined by the prevailing westerlies and the warm Japanese current, is near-Mediterranean in southern areas, a condition which has accounted for the considerable population of veterans in retirement. Racially, almost seventy per cent of the province is British in origin. But the earliest British visitors were stirred less by climate than by the brooding heights and crags and the wild torrents that recalled their native land; and it was fitting that a Scot, Simon Fraser from Glengarry, should have named the region New Caledonia, a nostalgic title which was retained until the monopoly of the Hudson's Bay Company was ended, and a separate mainland colony established in 1858.

The Fraser River, British Columbia.

Chapter Two

THE DISCOVERERS

'If men consider the divine work of God and the end of his working,' wrote that great Elizabethan, Admiral Sir William Monson, 'it is marvellous to behold that America, being a continent and equal to all the rest of the world in bigness, should be concealed from the creation till one thousand four hundred and ninety odd years after the birth of Christ, and not so much as imagined, though some philosophers seemed to rove at it.' More than three hundred years later, the question of who from the Old World first preceded Columbus on the eastern coast of the New had become the subject of furious debate.

Vikings

According to old and embroidered sagas handed down through the mists of time, and generally accepted by modern historians, the northern half of North America was first visited by Norsemen called Vikings. In the year 1000, Leif Ericsson, a Norwegian whose father had founded a settlement on the south-west coast of Greenland, was driven off his course by storms, to find refuge on what would appear to be the New England coast. Two or three years later he returned, sailing westward from Green-land to a bleak and barren shore which was probably northern Labrador; thence, southward round Newfoundland to a fairly flat and wooded coast, with stretches of white sand, Markland, which may well have been Nova Scotia, and finally to a Vinland of grain and wild grapes which, in the opinion of some experts, lay near Cape Cod.

35

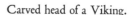
Carved head of a Viking.

But in recent years there have been plausible revisions of traditional history, which suggest that even before Leif Ericsson, primitive navigators crossed the Atlantic. As a result of exhaustive researches and re-examination of circumstantial evidence, mythical competitors have taken on life. It has been submitted, for instance, that Celtic monks, fleeing westward from the ravaging Vikings, moved first to Iceland, thence, by way of Greenland, to the Gulf of St Lawrence where they survived for several generations. Other authoritative challengers declare that America must have been discovered by voyagers from Africa. Conjectural controversy will almost certainly continue; one thing only remains beyond dispute: that brave Scandinavians did sail westward into the unknown wastes; some may have reappeared after months or years with tales of new lands; the fate of most will probably never be known.

Archaeological discovery supports the literary and cartographical evidence of their endeavours. Recent discoveries indicate that Norsemen established a colony on the northernmost tip of Newfoundland. Excavations completed in 1964 near L'Anse aux Meadows revealed dwelling-houses and other structures bearing striking similarities to habitations of the same period in Iceland, Greenland and Norway. Moreover, it is unlikely that later Europeans would have employed such primitive smelting methods as appear to have been used in a smithy which was unearthed on the same spot; neither Indians nor Eskimos, who frequented the area, could smelt or forge iron.

There is little evidence, however, to show how long the Norsemen stayed in Newfoundland, or whether they managed to penetrate inland. From their Greenland base, which was only about two hundred miles away, almost certainly they continued their explorations by sea. In 1007 an expedition of three vessels carrying one hundred and fifty men, a few women, livestock and stores appears to have reached the mainland of Labrador. But after three hard winters, those who survived cold, scurvy and native hostility returned to Greenland. Here the parent colony hung on until extinguished in the fifteenth century by pestilence and the Eskimos. So the curtain lifted by Leif Ericsson came down again to hide the continent that Columbus was to discover afresh on his way to the Indies.

This 72-foot Viking ship, known as the Gokstad Ship, is believed to have been the type used to cross the North Atlantic.

Long before Columbus' landfall made news, Portuguese and French sailors may have travelled westward to explore and fish off the Grand Banks. Either they kept their findings secret, or they may have been illiterate men who dispensed with records; certainly no word of their exploits leaked into the world's literary archives. In any event not until the end of the fifteenth century did such adventurers enter the pages of *John Cabot* English history to stake claims of empire. Giovanni Gabotto was a

The eroded coastline of Cape Breton Island, where John Cabot landed in 1497. With his sons Ludovicus, Sebastian (*right*) and Sanctus he was given authority by Henry VII of England in March 1496 to navigate in seas to the east, north or west, and to occupy 'any new lands hitherto unvisited by Christians'.

Venetian who emigrated to England, where he became naturalized as John Cabot. Debarred from sailing to the south because Spain controlled the seas, Cabot sailed north and west, and on 24 June 1497 landed probably on the extremity of Cape Breton Island, where he took possession of the country in the name of his patron Henry VII. His second voyage in the following year took him to the same general area, whence he coasted south-eastwards along Labrador and Newfoundland as far as

Chesapeake Bay. Considering the low quality of both ships and crew it was a triumph of navigation, but the results were meagre in terms of expectations. A few paltry cod-fish and furs were a poor substitute for the gold and silks that the Orient had promised. None the less, the labours of John Cabot and of his son, Sebastian, gave England legal pretension to an important sector of the Atlantic seaboard, which a century later she would attempt to colonize; and they advertised the riches of the Grand Banks, where schools of cod assembled in such numbers 'they sometimes stayed the ships'. Although no settlement was attempted on Newfoundland, thenceforward European fishing vessels came annually to make their catches near her forbidding shores. But more than thirty years were to elapse before Breton and Norman made ready to engrave their achievements for posterity.

There are still rich fishing grounds near barren Sugar Loaf Head, St John's, Newfoundland (*opposite*), as there were when fifteenth-century ships, such as the one shown (*left*), made their catches.

The early explorers had been generally Italian in origin. In a few years, however, the Atlantic fisheries were producing a tough and imaginative breed of French sailors, and it was from this nursery that a pilot from St *Cartier* Malo, Jacques Cartier, emerged as the real discoverer of Canada's mainland. In the spring of 1534, Cartier set out with two small vessels and 42 sixty men. Like Cabot before him, he headed due west to avoid the

1546 map of the east coast and the St Lawrence estuary showing the landing of Jacques Cartier and the first colonists.

Spaniards, intent on reaching Asia, but also hopeful of discovering new lands on the way. He reached Newfoundland in May, and thence, by way of the Strait of Belle Isle, entered the Gulf of St Lawrence, looking in vain for the passage that would lead him to the Pacific Ocean. In the following year, he tried again, and this time with remarkable skill brought his three ships up the great river of Canada some eight hundred miles as far as the present city of Quebec, where he appears to have been warmly welcomed by the Indian chief of 'Kannata'. Stirred by stories of a distant country 'in which are infinite rubies, gold and other riches', Cartier pushed on as far as Montreal (known to the Indians as Hochelaga), where further progress was barred by the Lachine Rapids. With the instinct of a practised sightseer, he climbed to the summit of the neigh-bouring mountain, 'which was named by us, Mont-Royal', and like Moses gazed upon the Promised Land. All around stretched the vast forest bounded by mountains to the north and to the south, and cutting through the background of flaming autumn leaves, the broad ribbon of the St Lawrence. 'As far as the eye can reach,' he wrote in his *Voyages,* 'one sees that river, large, wide and broad, which came from the south-west.'

Since the season was late – early October – Cartier returned to Quebec, where he spent a miserable winter, fearful of Indian attacks and harassed by deep frosts and blizzards from the north. Owing to lack of fruit and fresh vegetables scurvy spread rapidly among his crews, and by February the entire expedition seemed doomed. Of the seventy-four men from his own ship, twenty-five had died; only three or four were physically active. From this desperate plight he was saved by friendly Indians, who taught him how to make medicinal tea from the bark of the white spruce. This magic elixir undoubtedly saved the lives of men confined by tradition to a diet of biscuit and salt meat. '. . . in less than eight days,' wrote Cartier, 'a whole tree as tall as any I ever saw was consumed.'

The third expedition was delayed until 1541, when the King of France appointed Jean François de la Rocque, Sieur de Roberval, as viceroy of a New France that should rival New Spain. Lacking the co-operation of his reluctant subordinate, Cartier, Roberval's effort at colonization was a fiasco, and he was fortunate to reach his homeland again, in the summer of 1543, with a cargo of 'fool's gold' and stones like diamonds, subsequently shown to be worthless. France had failed to establish a northern base on the way to the East. Admittedly, severe cold, scurvy and Indians were serious obstacles to success, but in the light of future achievement, the French failure was chiefly one of manpower. The promoters of colonization preferred, like the first English settlers in

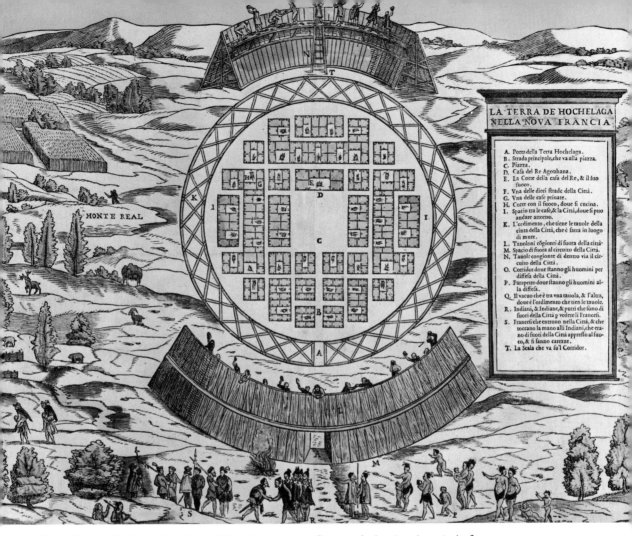

LA TERRA DE HOCHELAGA
NELLA NOVA FRANCIA.

A. Porta della Terra Hochelaga.
B. Strada principale, che va alla piazza.
C. Piazza.
D. Casa del Re Agouhana.
E. La Corte della casa del Re, & il suo fuoco.
F. Vna delle dieci strade della Città.
G. Vna delle case priuate.
H. Corte con il fuoco, doue si cucina.
I. Spacio tra le case, & la Città, doue si puo andare attorno.
K. L'ordimento, che tiene le tauole della citta della Città, che è fatta in luogo di mure.
L. Tauoloni cōgionti di fuora della città.
M. Spacio di fuora al circuito della Città.
N. Tauole congionte di dentro via il circuito della Città.
O. Corridor doue stanno gli huomini per diffesa della Città.
P. Parapetto doue stanno gli huomini alla diffesa.
Q. Il vacuo che è tra vna tauola, & l'altra, doue è l'ordimento che tien le tauole.
R. Indiani, & Indiane, & putti che sono di fuori della Città p vedere li Francesi.
S. Francesi che entrano nella Città, & che toccano la mano alli Indiani, che erano di fuori della Città appresso al fuoco, & si fanno carezze.
T. La Scala che va su'l Corridor.

Plan of the fortified Iroquois village of Hochelaga, the site of Montreal, showing the arrival of the French.

Virginia, to conduct operations with the sweepings of the streets and gaols, rather than with farmers and artisans who had the fibre to resist the rigours of the Canadian winter and the doggedness as well as the talent to live off the land.

Meanwhile, although Cartier appeared to have opened one gate on the road to Cathay, France was not interested in Canada. For more than sixty years, contact was maintained only through visiting fishermen who traded for beaver skins on the shores of the Gulf of St Lawrence. Yet these Basques and Bretons were the real precursors of French dominion. Just as

Fur Trade

45

The fur trade. Iroquois driving game into traps by striking bones together.

tobacco saved the first English colony in Virginia, so did the developing fur trade, in response to the European demand, resuscitate French colonization in the St Lawrence Valley. Admirably suited for felting, the beaver's pelt provided seventeenth-century Europe with the most fashionable gentleman's hat. And to satisfy this compelling fashion, the pioneers of great colonial powers pursued the animal along lake and river, through wilderness and across broad plains, over the mountains as far as the Pacific Ocean. In the course of this long chase, Frenchman fought Englishman and Iroquois killed Huron in order that trade routes should be safeguarded and colonial exchequers solvent.

For many years, however, the pursuit of the beaver remained incidental to the search for the North-West Passage. European courts wanted gold and silver even more than fur hats. In the days before the credit system simplified processes of international exchange, a Treasury well stocked in bullion was regarded as vital to a nation's stability and strength. Of this need, Drake's raids on Spanish-American towns and galleons are sufficient testimony. On the other hand, a state which was interested in becoming self-sufficient, and hence better secured against the hostility of neighbour or rival, sought independence not simply by hoarding precious metals, but by acquiring valuable commodities such as timber, masts, naval stores, potash for the woollen industry, fish and, of course, furs. Hakluyt reported for the benefit of the English on 'that part of America which lieth betweene 30 and 60 degrees of northerly latitude . . . all kinds of odiferous trees and date trees, cypresses, and cedars; and in New found lands aboundance of pines and firr trees to make mastes and deale boards, pitch, tar, rosen; hempe for cables and cordage; and upp within the Graunde Baye, excedinge quantitie of all kinde of precious furres.'

Elks on an Indian 'coat of arms'.

Like their contemporaries at Jamestown, the begetters of French settlement in Canada were much more interested in finding Eldorados than in exploiting the resources of land and river. Yet men who toiled for gold were eventually driven to till the soil to avoid starvation, and in the process they became colonizers. Within Canada, trade and exploration were never divorced from settlement, because the colony was required to pay its way; and since Canada turned out to be neither a Peru nor a Mexico, men who pursued the fur trade still dreamed of a short cut through an obstinate land mass that would lead them eventually to the fabulous wealth of the Orient.

The arms of the Hurons

The beaver (*below*), which played so vital a role in the early history of Canada, appears on a stamp of 1851 (*right*) and on an Indian 'coat of arms' (*right centre*).

47

At the beginning of the seventeenth century the size and shape of the North American continent were still unknown. Cartier had shown that the Gulf of St Lawrence was not an ocean strait leading directly to eastern seas, but the estuary of a mighty river, navigable for sea-going vessels only as far as the Lachine Rapids. None the less, might not the country to the north-west taper away into broken groups of islands, or at the worst a manageable isthmus? So argued a devout sailor from the village of Brouage in Saintonge (Charente-Maritime) who 'dreamed greatly' about the passage to the East which Martin Frobisher and John Davis and other distinguished navigators had failed to find.

Champlain   By any count, Samuel de Champlain remains the model explorer and pioneer. 'His character', wrote Francis Parkman, the greatest of North American historians, 'belonged partly to the past, partly to the present. The *preux chevalier*, the crusader, the romance-loving explorer, the curious knowledge-seeking traveller, the practical navigator, all claimed

Martin Frobisher (*left*) was accompanied on part of his voyage north of the Hudson Strait by the English artist John White, who drew this encounter with Eskimos.

Samuel de Champlain, 1608.

their share in him. His views, though far beyond those of the mean spirits around him, belonged to his age and his creed.' No Englishman of that age, not even among the Elizabethans, was so imbued with the imperial ideal. But empire-builders whatever their race or creed were not always good men. Champlain was eminently a righteous man of faith and courage, whose weaknesses were those of the idealist and visionary. To the very last he held to his purpose 'to sail beyond the sunset and the baths of all the western stars'.

Shortly after he had established his first trading post in 1608 on the present site of Quebec, he organized a small expedition to ascend the St Lawrence in the hope that some northerly tributary might lead him to the open sea and China. Even when the continent grew wider before his eyes, his dream simply broadened to include an empire tapped by a great vestibule of Eastern commerce. As late as 1613 he sought this route by canoe and on foot, encouraged by the testimony of an irresponsible romancer, Nicolas Vignaud, who claimed to have reached the Western Sea by way of the Ottawa River. With the exposure of the fraud, Champlain's hopes were dashed. The prospect of ultimate fulfilment never ceased to occupy him, but henceforward his main energies were bent to the task of nourishing his fragile settlement.

In 1604, under the auspices of the Sieur de Monts, the French had experimented with a settlement on the Bay of Fundy. Three years later,

49

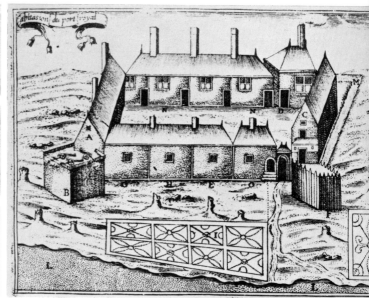

A Logemens des artisans.
B Plate forme où estoit le canon.
C Le magasin.
D Logemét du sieur dePont-graué & Champlain.
E La forge.

F Palissade de pieux.
G Le four.
H La cuisine.
O Petite maisonnette où l'on retiroit les vtansiles de nos barquesjque puis le sieur de Poittincourt fit

rebastir, & y logea le sieur Boulay quand le sieur du Pont s'en reuint en France.
P La porte de l'abitation.
Q Le cemetiere.
R La riuiere.

N ij

The *Habitations* of Port Royal and Quebec,
from Champlain's *Voyages*, 1613.

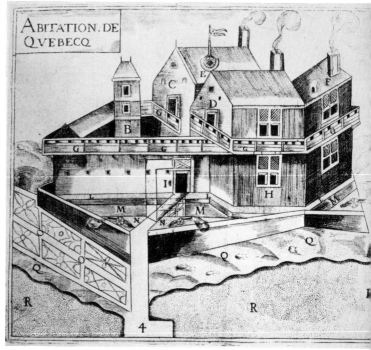

A Le magazin.
B Colombier.
C Corps de logis où sont nos armes, & pour loger les ouriers.
D Autre corps de logis pour les ouriers.
E Cadran.
F Autre corps de logis où est la forge, & artisans logés.
G Galleries tout au tour des

logemens.
H Logis du sieur de Champlain.
I La porte de l'habitation, où il y a Pont-leuis.
L Promenoir autour de l'habitation contenant 10. pieds de large iusques sur le bort du fossé.
M Fossés tout autour de l'habitation.

N Plattes formes, en façon de tenailles pour mettre le canon.
O Iardin du sieur de Champlain.
P La cuisine.
Q Place deuant l'habitation sur le bort de la riuiere.
R La grande riuiere de sainct Lorens.

50

however, Champlain fixed on Quebec rather than Port-Royal as the main base. Quebec seemed eminently suited to be not only a strategic *point d'appui* on the projected route to the East, but the pivotal trading post for the fur trade. Once the initial phase of digging in was over, and the settlers assured of a subsistence and shelter, he realized that the beaver would have to be hunted systematically, otherwise the colony could not survive. 'Precious furres', as Hakluyt called them, were as vital to the colonial economy as bullion to the French government in Paris.

Hitherto, the fur trade had been open to anyone with sufficient enterprise and stamina to face the climate, the ruthless competition of rival adventurers and the Indians. Some form of regulation was obviously necessary, and Champlain started the system of company monopolies, which under Richelieu's auspices culminated in a great national organization, popularly known as the Company of the One Hundred

Champlain's map of the New England coast. The Bay of Fundy in the north-east is marked 'La baye française'; the French settlement of Port-Royal is on the south shore of the bay.

Hurons in
aboriginal dress
(*above and far right*);
this tribe were
supported by
Champlain.

Associates. This body, which included nobles and influential merchants, was entrusted, in 1627, with the government of the colony and
the control of its trade for fifteen years on condition that some three
hundred colonists were brought out each year. Such an authority was
necessary not only to stiffen the colony, but to protect an investment
which depended finally on good relations with the Indian hunters.
Unhappily, in 1609 Champlain had made the fateful decision to ally
himself with the Hurons of the Ottawa and the Algonkins of the St
Lawrence Valley. More numerous than their enemies the Iroquois who
lived in the country south of Lake Ontario, they were far less able
warriors, and in subsequent years the alliance was to bring the colony
to the verge of destruction.

Champlain has often been blamed by historians for a grave error in
judgment. He was aware as early as 1603 of Iroquois power, but he
could not foretell the consequences of its deadly impact; and even if he
had shown unique prescience, he could scarcely have avoided taking
sides. Because they controlled the neighbouring river routes to the westward fur-bearing areas, the Hurons and Algonkins were strategically
placed as natural allies. In similar fashion, geography had cast the acquisitive Iroquois Confederacy, to the south of the Great Lakes, as natural
rivals of the French in the St Lawrence Valley, just as it made them
potential allies of the neighbouring English and Dutch settlements. Given
sufficient strength, the French were theoretically in a position to command
a continuous river and lake system to the heart of the continent; but the
line of communication was long and vulnerable. From bases on the
Hudson and Mohawk rivers, from Lake Champlain and by the Richelieu River, the English with their Iroquois allies were in a position to
interrupt or cut the main highway of their competitors, and thus strangle
the French colony.

For twenty years, beginning in the 1640s, with a ferocity beyond
comparison in primitive warfare, the Iroquois ravaged the line of French
settlement along the St Lawrence as far as Quebec, coming close to
paralysing the fur trade. Had the government in Paris supported Champlain at the outset with men and arms, the danger might have been
eliminated before it had a chance to develop under the stimulus of English

f. 15

Cet Jcy vn —
depute du bourg de gannachiou
avé pouvAlles inuites au Jeu les
Missieurs de gandaouyadga.
Jls tiennent que le ser portent
le dieu du peuple linnoquent
le tenant en main en dansant
et chantant.

Indian of the Iroquois tribe.

firearms, trade goods and rum. Only if the Iroquois had been crushed or neutralized was Canada in a position to retain the alliance of western tribes on whose industry the life of the colony depended. It is interesting to speculate on the future of France in North America had there been no powerful Iroquois Confederacy. Conceivably, French settlement behind French troops would have moved southward down the Hudson River towards warmer weather and a winter seaport at New York. It was France's misfortune that Canadian history did not, like Australian history, begin with an empty continent. In North America, the presence of the Indian governed not only the pace of European settlement, but the fortunes of rival European powers for more than a century.

The French, with their Huron and Algonkin allies (E), about to destroy the Iroquois stockade (A). Champlain and his French companions are marked D and F; on the left an Indian (H) is chopping down a tree which will fall on the stockade. *Above,* Champlain fixing his arquebus.

In terms of economic growth, the Indian was indispensable in the repeated stages of frontier expansion which saw the fur trade expand from the St Lawrence Valley westward across the plains to the Rocky Mountains and beyond. He was also during the earlier period of contact, the subject of passionate missionary zeal on the part of the French. Unlike the Spaniards or the French, the English had rarely a sense of religious mission, although stern resolution and fortitude were frequently buttressed by strong faith. The French had the same qualities of courage and endurance, but in addition they possessed an unusual skill in native diplomacy which was frequently associated with missionary enterprise. Champlain certainly envisaged his project of empire as one that should include the conversion of heathen tribes to the glory of God and the Church and the honour of France.

Jesuit   In Champlain's mind, missions and the fur trade went hand in hand.
Explorers In terms of government and Company policy, conversion took second place to profits, but it would be an error to assume that charter obligations to Christianize the natives were merely a form of lip-service as practised by the English to the south. Unlike the Sulpicians and Récollets, the Jesuits did have a hand in the fur trade, but the incidental barter of European goods for peltries scarcely justified the strictures of earlier historians against an Order which has been under attack throughout most of its history. Indeed, its record in Canada is one of nobility, dedication and incredible fearlessness. No one can listen to the tortured cries of Father Jean de Brébeuf and his comrades without recognizing a loyalty that extended far beyond the state. 'The grandeur of their self-devotion', wrote Parkman, one of their severest critics, 'towers conspicuously over all.'

The Jesuit *Relations*, or narratives, which were widely circulated in France, provide one of the principal sources of seventeenth-century Canadian history. Some of them are as weighted with references to the prospect of eternal damnation as any Puritan tract; many of them are long and repetitive chronicles of piety and mystical ecstasy; but others are as rich in adventure as any of the novels of Fenimore Cooper or Zane Grey. There are hair-breadth escapes in river and rapids, tales of endurance on woodland trails, and also warm and human stories of pioneer life, of

Jesuit missions among the Hurons were brought to an end by Iroquois attacks in which several Jesuits and hundreds of Hurons were killed. This engraving shows the martyrdom in 1648 of Father Brébeuf and his companions.

beasts and birds and fertile forest glades awaiting the axe or the plough of the immigrant, and always in the background beyond the clearing, the lurking terror of the Iroquois.

Few of the Jesuits came from the humbler classes of French society; the vanguard, which came out in 1625, consisted largely of sensitive men of culture, intellectual quality and sometimes of noble birth, who had, in many instances, relinquished comfortable posts at home to share a savage native existence in the wilderness. They lived through icy winters and the sweltering heat of summers; they suffered the nausea of daily life in

Indian villages, with the smoke, the fleas, the dirt, the stench and the scanty and unaccustomed food. Yet they managed to build the rough-hewn church, succour the ailing, baptize the dying, all too often sealing their devotion with their lives under excruciating torture.

Brébeuf died by slow burning at the hands of the Iroquois in 1649. The spiritual purpose that took him from a gentle Norman background, and led him through every ordeal to the final trial shines out still amid the welter of this world's savagery. St Ignace, the scene of his martyrdom, lies on the east bank of the Sturgeon River, near Midland, Ontario, the centre of the area known as Huronia, a peninsula of rolling hills and thick forests thrusting north into Georgian Bay. When the Récollet, Father Joseph Le Caron, first visited the region it was inhabited by some thirty thousand Hurons, one of the largest concentrations of Indian population north of Mexico.

The tragedy of Huronia may appear to lie outside the main stream of events that witnessed the establishment of French power in North America. Yet the Jesuit effort was not unrelated to French colonial destiny. France, on the initiative of Champlain, wanted to develop a strong Catholic Indian protectorate, a bulwark against the spread of English influence, capable of safeguarding the colony against Iroquois aggression, and providing the nucleus of an empire in the heart of the continent. The Jesuits were, in short, the spearhead of an imperial crusade aimed at securing the focal areas of the fur trade against the menace of the Iroquois Confederacy and the ambitions of their allies, the English. A Huron nation welded to the French faith and buttressed by French arms could dominate the main lines of communication and trade that led south to the Mississippi Valley and, north of Lake Superior, to the far west. The virtual extinction of Huronia and the Huron race by the middle of the seventeenth century signalled not only the failure of a mission, but a desperate crisis in the fortunes of New France.

In fact, long before disaster overtook the Hurons, the French colony in Canada seemed destined to go the way of its predecessor, Port Royal. Twenty years after the founding of Quebec its population numbered only sixty-five persons, of whom only twenty were adult males. And in that year, 1628, when Richelieu's Company of One Hundred Associates sent

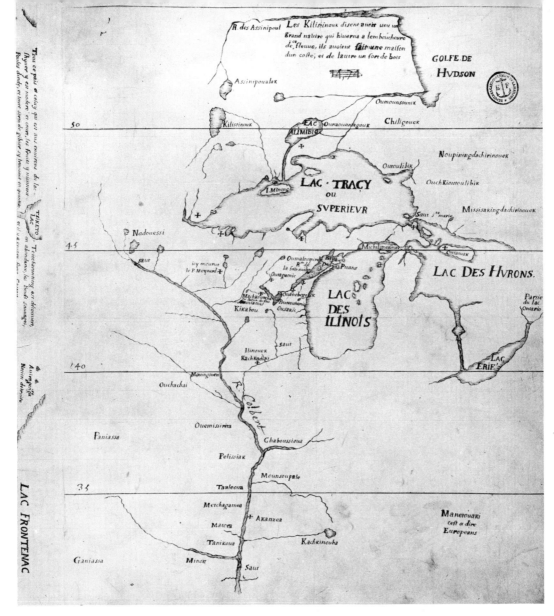

Jesuits took a leading part in exploration. This Jesuit travelling map of 1682 shows the regions between the Mississippi (Colbert) River and Lake Ontario. The crosses indicate places where priests died.

out their first reinforcements – eighteen vessels containing farmers, priests and artisans, along with food supplies and implements, arms and ammunition – the expedition ran straight into the clutches of a small English privateering squadron commanded by David Kirke. A few months later, a starving settlement was compelled to surrender.

Quebec was returned to the French in 1632 under the Treaty of St Germaine-en-Laye, and Champlain faced the painful task of pulling the pieces together. But the Company which promised more men and supplies had lost enthusiasm. The cost of finding, exporting and maintaining suitable colonists had always cut heavily into profits from the fur trade. Immigration dropped to a trickle, and the founder of New France was no longer equal to fighting his cause in the French court. Worn out by his sisyphean labours Champlain died in Quebec on Christmas Day, 1635, at the age of sixty-eight.

That the colony was saved in this extremity was owing chiefly to Jesuit propaganda. Men and women of wealth and influence who had read the *Relations* and been stirred by the appeals of heroic missionaries, joined together to form Canada's first immigration agency – the Society of Our Lady of Montreal. In the summer of 1641, the first contingent of forty-seven souls under the leadership of a zealous Christian soldier, the Sieur de Maisonneuve, set out for the island of Montreal, which the Society had obtained by official grant. Situated at the junction of the Ottawa and the St Lawrence, this outpost of French civilization was soon to become the focal centre of the fur trade and a strategic bastion of New France. For the next twenty years its inhabitants were to sustain with immense gallantry the main weight of ferocious and relentless Indian warfare that extended to the new settlement at Three Rivers and as far as Quebec.

Marguerite Bourgeoys (1620–1700)
founder of the Society of Our Lady of Montreal
to convert and teach the Indians,
joined Maisonneuve in Montreal in 1653.

Chapter Three

Canada was not a country that could be easily settled. The Spaniards had been lucky. In the Caribbean they had been favoured by soil and climate. There were, of course, certain handicaps in the shape of noxious fevers and tropical heat; but, on the whole, the environment was genial; the products of the soil were many and easily procurable, and the natives, as compared with the Iroquois, were children. In Canada the situation was almost reversed. The French faced bitter winters; for more than five months of the year, farming came to a dead stop, and ice in the great St Lawrence River blocked communication between Quebec and France. Moreover, they suffered under the constant assaults of a vindictive Indian Confederacy, which threatened to extinguish the entire colony. During the last months of 1661 no fewer than eighty Frenchmen had been killed or captured in the neighbourhood of their own farms.

The miracle is that French settlement should have survived at all. By 1663, out of a population of some sixteen million (double that of England, which had sent some forty thousand emigrants to the New England coast) France had been able to provide Canada with only 2,500 settlers, most of whom were confined to three small settlements at Quebec, Three Rivers and Montreal. The population of Acadia amounted to less than four hundred, mainly in Port Royal, with remnants scattered among half a dozen fishing stations along the shores of the Annapolis Basin. Indeed,

French
Settlement

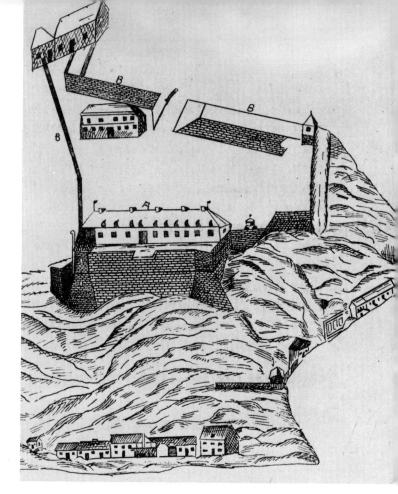

The Marquis de Tracy.

Plan of Fort St Louis, Quebec, in 1683. The original château is marked (A), the outer wall which was begun in 1683 and razed in 1693 (B).

Acadia remained a forlorn waif, unattended by France, vulnerable to English sea power and destitute of protection against the fumbling raids of Massachusetts militiamen, who were already assaulting her mouldering forts and sacking diminutive hamlets.

As it happened, Louis XIV was determined to save his feeble possessions overseas by bringing them under direct control. On 30 June 1665, two ships came to anchor below the Rock in the Basin of Quebec. From the mast of the larger vessel floated the royal standard of France. From the bastion of St Louis cannon thundered out a welcome, as the Lieutenant-General of all the King's possessions in North America, the Marquis de Tracy, stepped on the quay, followed by a number of young

Louis XIV.

noblemen bent on winning laurels in the New World. In his train, too, came detachments of the regiment of Carignan-Salières, the first regular troops ever to be sent to Canada. This famous regiment had served with distinction in the Austrian war against the Turks; now they were to raise the colony's prestige socially, and to perform with professional *élan* against the Iroquois. When their tour of duty was over, many of them, officers as well as men, were persuaded to settle on the banks of the Richelieu River, the enemy's principal highway into Canada.

The day of Company charters was over; interested only in the fur trade, shareholders and directors had been unwilling to spend money either to defend the colony or to populate it. Apart from missionary priests

Jean-Baptiste Colbert.

and the occasional adventurer, immigration had practically ceased, and it was seriously proposed to make the unhappy land a dumping-ground for hardened criminals. Now, all was changed. By introducing a Sovereign Council composed of governor, bishop and intendant, along with four local residents, Louis' chief minister Colbert had laid the foundations of a permanent colonial bureaucracy responsible to the King.

Administration

Under this new regime, the governor as administrative head was mainly responsible for military affairs; the bishop, although in theory confined to the ecclesiastical, not infrequently found the moral welfare of

64

the community a problem requiring political action. The intendant dealt chiefly with economic, financial and judicial matters. Unlike the English colonies to the south, there were no local assemblies or municipal bodies to annoy or hamper the work of the central administration. The government was essentially a benevolent dictatorship. On the other hand, strife between a strong governor and an ambitious intendant could strain the machinery to breaking-point, and there were dramatic moments when a powerful bishop threatened to turn the colony into a theocracy.

But once royal intervention had produced solvency and comparative security, the colony ceased to be a precarious experiment; it had become a fact. During the next thirty years, a programme of state-aided immigration and subsidized industrial development led to a tenfold expansion of the original settlements. In the light of recent debility it was an astonishing recovery, and it was owing very largely to the inspiration and drive of an intendant, Jean Talon, who, in an age more conspicuous for knavery than self-sacrifice, carried out to the full the wishes of his government.

Jean Talon, Intendant of New France.

As king-pin of the administrative machinery, Talon's chief task was to build up population. Since Champlain's day, males had obviously predominated, but in the new era of stability, it was essential that every settler should have a wife and rear a family. Marriage became, therefore, a matter not of inclination but of duty. The bachelor received no sympathy from government, and single blessedness was soon the subject of heavy penalties. Talon arranged for the shipment of potential brides, and on their arrival reluctant males were given fifteen days to conduct courtship and seal a partnership. In these circumstances, it is understandable that a certain amount of scrimmaging occurred at the docks. Occasionally the ships brought dubious characters, who were promptly returned to France, but most of the immigrants were *demoiselles bien choisies*, of good health and good will, a mixture of middle-class and peasant stock, capable apparently of standing comparison in charm and sturdiness with the original *jolies brunettes canadiennes* already acclimatized to pioneer life.

As a result of Talon's campaign, by the end of the century the population had increased to seven thousand, the area of cultivated land had doubled, and new industries had been launched. And under the *Laval* guidance of the most powerful prelate in Canadian history, François de Laval, the foundations were laid for a Canadian clergy. The Seminary which he established at Quebec was to become in 1852 the University of Laval.

Bishop Laval was an autocratic puritan, with an almost fanatical belief in the justice of his various causes. Not infrequently he was on the side of the righteous. With tooth and nail he fought to stop the sale of traders' brandy which, at the cost of debauching the natives, expedited the inflow of furs at low prices. To abolish brandy as an article of barter, argued Laval's opponents, would simply mean diverting the fur trade to the English, with no ultimate benefit to the susceptible Indian, who was equally happy to accept rum. *Raison d'état* denied all compromise, and despite spasmodic efforts at regulation, the traffic in spirits was to ravage tribal populations from Hudson Bay southward and westward to the Pacific.

But whether it happened to be the brandy question, the riotous behaviour of irresponsible *coureurs-de-bois* or the private life of a govern-

François de Montmorency-Laval,
first Bishop of New France.

ment official, Laval was bound by his nature to become the turbulent
priest. Had he been less fanatical in his behaviour, he might have brought
a much-needed discipline into colonial life; but against Louis de Buade,
Comte de Frontenac, the most theatrical, irascible and arrogant governor
in Canadian history, the proponent of theocratic authority was bound to
suffer defeat. The Iroquois were a greater danger to the community than
brandy, Gallicanism or adultery. Louis XIV backed the tempestuous
soldier and recalled the bishop.

Today the soldier-hero of one of Parkman's most absorbing narratives
is under a cloud. Modern historians have shown Frontenac to be a rapa-
cious trader who dealt in smuggled furs, and an impetuous tactician
whose bloody forays into the Iroquois country served no enduring
strategic purpose. None the less, in time of need this strange, impulsive
nobleman, who had ruined a career at court by his uncontrollable
temper, breathed some of his own fiery energy into an anaemic colony
that had lived continuously on the defensive. However misjudged his
military policy of border reprisals, it was Frontenac who first broke the
Iroquois-English alliance.

67

That French dominion in North America lasted as long as it did was partly owing to the presence of the well-trained professional troops, and partly to the hierarchical structure of administration which extended in pyramid fashion from governor and intendant in Quebec downward to the broad-based network of feudal land tenures and feudal service, known as the seigneurial system. The wisdom of transferring from France to the New World 'this antiquated relic of medievalism' has often been questioned, and it is true that the military aspect of seigneurial service had died out, as French kings concentrated more and more power in Paris. But the method of land tenure, while in decline, persisted as the basis of the French social structure, and it was perfectly natural, and also sensible, to graft this controlled, yet flexible system on frontier society in Canada.

The origins of the seigneurial system can be traced back to 1598 when the Sieur de la Roche was commissioned as Lieutenant-General of all the dominions claimed by France in North America, and given authority to establish a hierarchy of landowners. Roche's attempt at colonization was a failure, but the founder of Quebec, Champlain, was allowed to begin the experiment. Unfortunately, as we have seen, successive Company directors were more interested in the fur trade than in settlement, and lack of consistent support from home, combined with recurring Indian invasions, meant that only some sixty grants had been made by 1663. The systematic development of the seigneurial method had to await the coming of Talon.

The seigneuries were normally situated along the shores of the St Lawrence and Richelieu rivers. Grants were made in wide strips containing anything from fifty to several hundred acres, with waterfronts of three to seven miles. In return for a pledge of fealty to the King, and an undertaking to perform military service, the seigneur received his concession without money payment, and held it so long as he carried out his obligation of clearing the land within a prescribed time. Consequently, he was dependent on his tenants (usually twelve to fifteen in a seigneury), to whom he sub-let divisions of perhaps one hundred or as much as two hundred and fifty acres. The tenant had complete security of possession so long as he paid a nominal rent and performed the necessary tasks required of a pioneer farmer. On the other hand, he could sell out, or buy

French Canadian
gentilhomme
with snowshoes.

another tenancy at will. He was no serf who changed with the land, but a free *habitant* – a 'dweller on the soil' – with a real and not a nominal independence.

The seigneur himself was a kind of squire without political powers and without significant social status. He was usually a *gentilhomme*, a militia officer or a middle-class professional type who hoped to better his family prospects by digging roots in a new land. He was head of the local community, which he was expected to build up around the seigneury, and, as local magistrate, the guardian of its law and order. If he were an able man, the *habitants* looked to him for guidance and comfort in times of peril when Iroquois lurked in the cornfields or the more distant woods.

But he was never a landlord in the social and proprietary sense. Disgruntled tenants could sue him, and, if unsatisfied, could appeal directly to the central administration in Quebec.

In short, the Canadian *habitant* was not the down-trodden *censitaire* of old France. He paid his seigneur various rents and dues, but they were not oppressive, and were frequently offered in kind. The Abbé Casgrain has described how the seigneur, every autumn as Michaelmas approached, stood at the church door after Mass, to warn the congregation that their *cens et rentes* were shortly payable. And on the appointed day they arrived at the manor-house, some in carry-alls, some in sleighs, 'each bringing with him a chicken or two, oats by the bushel, or other products of his land. Sometimes the canny Norman would pay in grain or fowl when prices were low, and in money when prices were high, but more often the seigneur insisted in the deed that he should choose the method of payment.' With all the drink and tobacco and gossip and gaiety, the event seems to have been much like a barn-raising bee of recent times.

Although the *habitant* did have to grind his grain at the seigneur's mill and pay him one-fourteenth of the proceeds, from all accounts the seigneur was the loser, since he had to pay the miller's salary and maintain the mill. As for forced labour – the notorious *corvée* – it usually amounted to little more than a week's unpaid work a year; and it was not inappropriate in a harassed and mutually dependent society that settlers should co-operate to build and maintain roads and bridges and help each other in seed-time and harvest.

Like the seigneur, the *habitant* preferred to have his hundred or so acres on the river, and since his property was by tradition equally divided among his children, in course of time the strips grew narrower and narrower, and the little houses by the waterfront closer and closer together. At the end of the seventeenth century the St Lawrence River between Quebec and Montreal must have looked like a straggling village street. Some of that glamour still lingers. As his ship rounds the Point of Orleans, and passes below the rock fortress of Cape Diamond, crowned with the turrets of the Château Frontenac, the traveller finds himself ascending the avenue of the pioneers between rich pastures and woodlands marked at intervals with squat white houses, interspersed every few

A French-Canadian whitewashed house. Villeneuve House, Charlebourg, Quebec, which was built *c.* 1700.

miles with churches and the occasional refurbished 'mansion', conceivably the site of an old manor-house. Far beyond the ribboned farms, standing out in bold relief at sunset, rise the Laurentians, sloping gently towards the river below.

There were no châteaux on the St Lawrence or the Richelieu rivers. Indeed, the average seigneur's whitewashed dwelling was sometimes indistinguishable, save in size, from the tenant's one-storey log-cabin, with a garret for the children. Only rarely did the seigneurial home become a centre of community life; that position of social prestige and authority was occupied by the church.

In the earlier days of river settlements, the religious needs of the inhabitants had been met by roving priests who made their pastoral journeys in canoes. But by the time Talon left the colony, little churches were springing up, and around them parochial associations began to take shape. The parish fulfilled the function of a local municipality, whose principal civilian executive (officially the agent of the intendant) was the captain of militia. But the curé was the central link in parochial life, the friend and counsellor of the *habitant*, and subsequently, after the Conquest, his protector.

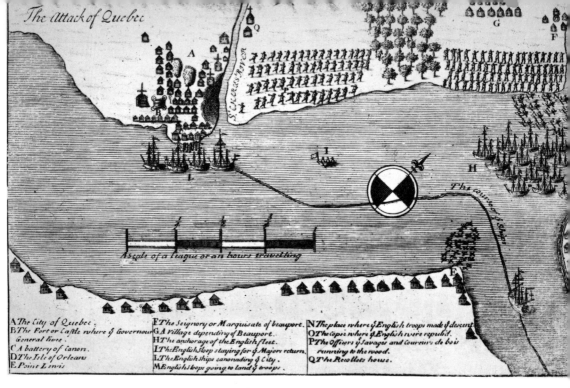

The Attack of Quebec

A scale of a league or an hours travelling

Sir William Phips's unsuccessful attack on Quebec in 1690 is shown above.

This drawing of 1740 shows the Upper Town of Quebec dominating the port.

72

All told, the parish scarcely represented an egalitarian society, but despite occasional squabbling over boundaries and *rentes* it was a neigh⁄bourly society. The close alignments of population along the river⁄banks, most within range of maurauding savages from the south, encouraged co⁄operation and promoted, or at least gave the feeling of, greater security. Unfortunately, this comforting proximity was at the expense of efficient farming. The seigneurial strips that stretched far back to the woods were so distant from house and barn that the *habitant* usually chose to scrape an existence on the few acres that were conveniently and more safely within reach. Not until the beginning of the eighteenth century did agriculture overcome traditional handicaps to become the stable basis of colonial society.

Quebec was the heart of the colony – a fortified stronghold whose artificial defences had begun to crumble long before the Boston militia under Sir William Phips made their futile assault on the Rock in 1690. Quebec was a seaport town and capital, with churches, parks, docks, *Fortress Quebec*

warehouses and substantial public buildings. In the Upper Town, which stretched back from the great rock cliff, stood the residence of the governor, the Château St Louis; also the bishop's palace, the cathedral and the Convent of the Ursulines, all enclosed by a protective stone wall breached by three imposing gates. Within these picturesque ramparts, the governor, supported by his staff and the chief civil and military officers, held court as near as possible in the style and manner of Paris or Versailles. Although the wealthier seigneur and his wife who came to the capital for the 'winter season' encountered little of the luxury and fantasy, they must have found something of the gaiety and colour that graced the exclusive circles of the élite at home.

The eighteenth-century historian Father Charlevoix concluded with pardonable exaggeration that social life at the beginning of the eighteenth century was not without intellectual and physical stimulus. 'There is a little select society here, which wants nothing to make it agreeable. In the salons of the wives of the Intendant and the Governor one finds circles as brilliant as in other countries. Everybody does his part to make the time pass pleasantly with games and pleasure parties. In the summer, drives and canoe excursions; in winter, skating and sleighing. The news of the day amounts to very little indeed as the country furnishes scarcely any, while that from Europe comes all at once. Science and the fine arts have their turn, and conversation does not fail. The Canadians breathe from their birth an air of liberty which makes them very pleasant in the intercourse of life, and our language is nowhere more purely spoken.'

The peasant folk who came to New France during the seventeenth and eighteenth centuries were robust, courageous and often enterprising, but unlike the governing élite who infrequently came to settle, they had little education. Consequently, there was none of the wide intellectual curiosity that pervaded the Thirteen Colonies, and which was helping to produce Benjamin Franklins before the Seven Years War. No printing press was set up during the Old Régime; no books were printed either in Acadia or Canada between the foundation of Port Royal in 1605 and the conquest of 1760. As late as 1785 only one in five could read, a condition which improved only slowly, and which helps to explain Lord Durham's unsympathetic judgment some fifty years later. 'There can

The first Ursuline Convent in Quebec, founded for works of charity.

hardly be conceived a nationality', he wrote in 1839, 'more destitute of all that can invigorate and elevate a people.'

But if the Old Régime produced few men of ideas, it at least provided *The Frontier* many men of action. Up-river, beyond the petty squabbles and corruption that contaminated the capital, the *habitant*, and the young seigneur too, were exposed to strange and exhilarating temptations in the freedom of the woods. It was this peculiarly Canadian frontier ethos that fashioned the *coureur-de-bois*.

The lure of furs encouraged exploration of the backwoods. This 1738 engraving of a beaver-hunt was probably done from the imagination. Other abundant animals sought for fur were the moose (*below left*) and the elk (*below right*).

In the early days, privileged traders had been content to let the Indians bring their furs to trading posts on the St Lawrence; later on, as the beaver retreated westward adventurous young men poured into the back-woods in search of wealth and excitement. Government regulations were no barrier to people who were bored with the humdrum life of the farm, and averse to any form of regimentation. Official decrees and Church mandates simply made outlaws of individuals whom the colony could ill

Early eighteenth-century impressions of the Canadian Indians and their way of life.

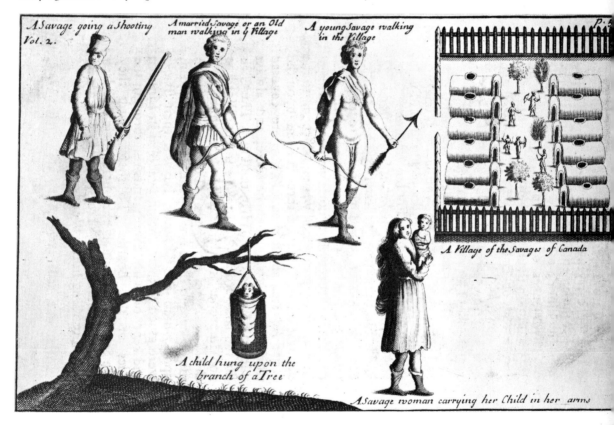

A Savage going a Shooting Vol. 2.

A married Savage or an Old man walking in y Village

A young Savage walking in the Village

A Village of the Savages of Canada

A child hung upon the branch of a Tree

A Savage woman carrying her Child in her arms

The explorer Father Louis Hennepin and his companions were captured by the Sioux in April 1680 near the mouth of the Wisconsin River while assisting La Salle in the exploration of the Mississippi Valley. The Indians

afford to lose. Many of them went native, taking Indian wives and making themselves part of the Indian community. Fearful of returning home, they sold their furs to the Dutch or English, or, equally illegally, to unscrupulous French agents who managed to avoid the twenty-five per cent tax. There can be no doubt that leading officials were involved in this illicit

78

Robert Cavelier, Sieur de La Salle, trader and explorer, discoverer of the mouths of the Mississippi in 1682, dreamed of a French empire to include the St Lawrence-Great Lakes basin and the Mississippi Valley as far as the Gulf of Mexico.

stole their vestments, fought over rolls of tobacco and showed fright at the sight of the glittering chalice. *Right*, Hennepin at Niagara Falls in 1679; this is the first published view of the Falls.

trade. By 1680 some six hundred *coureurs-de-bois* were on the advancing frontier, moving steadily westward over river and lake.

Meanwhile, French explorers cut pathways over the Great Shield, or paddled southward in the direction of the Gulf of Mexico. In 1658 Radisson and Groseilliers appear to have made contact with the Sioux

79

Indians of the western plains; three years later they reached James Bay. In 1673 Jolliet and Marquette entered the Mississippi over the low watershed dividing it from the St Lawrence basin, tracing portages for La Salle, Tonty and Hennepin, who followed the river as far as its mouth. In their wake, lightly garrisoned trading posts sprang up, until a loose network covered the main strategic points within the fur-bearing country between the Ohio River and the upper Mississippi. The Iroquois had been outflanked, and the English were in process of being hemmed in.

Such a hazardous policy of encirclement never received whole-hearted endorsement by the French government; yet the claims of French explorers were never countermanded, and as long as Frontenac was governor he never ceased to urge the necessity of blocking English access to the Ohio Valley. It was a grand project of empire that could never become a reality. A colony whose slender resources were consumed in the maintenance of communication lines from Labrador to Lake Superior, and along the maze of tributary streams that fed the Ohio and Mississippi rivers, was in no position to fulfil the vision of its imperial designers.

Nevertheless, the explorers, fur traders and missionaries who marked great avenues of commerce leading to the heart of North America were the creators of a legend, a legend that was to haunt their descendants long after the forest had been cleared from the lake shores, the sailing vessel supplanted by the steamer, and wilderness trails replaced by macadam roads and steel rails. Fashioned by the frontier, these men were also the progenitors of a separate species. If the Englishman, Dutchman or Scot who was slowly pushing through the foothills into the Appalachian Valley was becoming an American, similarly the Frenchman carving a home on the banks of the Richelieu, or pressing westward into the interior was in process of becoming a Canadian.

Chapter Four

THE CONQUERORS

In 1713 the population of New France was under twenty thousand; by then, more than twenty times as many English, Scottish and Irish emigrants had packed themselves into the Atlantic coastal strip east of the Appalachian mountain chain, and the great Anglo-Saxon population movements were only beginning. Against such overwhelming weight of numbers, nourished from the homeland by superior sea power, New France had little chance of survival. Although unrecognized at the time, the beginning of the eighteenth-century wars for empire saw the twilight of French dominion in North America.

The frequent border raids and counter-raids that took place between 1688 and 1713 had no bearing on the final outcome. When Frontenac relieved his feelings by ravaging the New England frontier, Massachusetts retaliated by sending an inexperienced eccentric, William Phips, to capture Port Royal, and in the same year, 1690, to assault Quebec. Frontenac had little difficulty in repulsing the invaders, but it was not without significance than an English force had been able to ascend the treacherous river and reach Quebec unscathed. English command of the sea meant that Canada's capital could be isolated at will from its mother country.

Quebec was to be saved again in 1711, when a 'courtier's expedition' under Sir Hovenden Walker was wrecked on the north shore of the St

The Hudson's Bay Company, founded in 1670, was granted its charter by Charles II, whose portrait (*above*) appears on the document.

Lawrence. It happened to be the first substantial operation directed against Canada from across the Atlantic. Faulty leadership contributed to its failure, but inept command scarcely concealed the weakness of British colonial organization. The advantages of overwhelming numbers had not been utilized to offset the strength which the French derived from professionally trained troops under feudal control.

Hudson's Bay Company   Meanwhile, on the frozen roof of the world, competition for the beaver country around James and Hudson Bay developed into a test of endurance and cunning. In 1670 Charles II had granted to the Hudson's Bay Company all the land drained by waters flowing into the Bay and Straits, an area amounting to more than a quarter of the continent. But France was equally interested. French ambitions reflected the same

The Hudson's Bay Company built fortified posts
such as Fort Nelson (York Factory), which is
shown here being taken by the French in 1697.

imperial zeal in the Northland as in the Mississippi Valley; the flag was
bound to follow the trade. On the other hand, the Bay shores were not an
object of territorial conquest; possession simply meant the establishment
of a few fortified posts for the benefit of the fur trade. Consequently, naval
warfare became a matter of surprise raids and landing parties, and since
the English posts were badly fortified and poorly garrisoned, victory
generally went to the French who put forth the greater effort. By 1713 only
Fort Albany on James Bay remained in English hands. Not on the sea,
but round the council table of the peacemakers, was Hudson Bay eventually regained for Britain, and it was a happy coincidence that the
European triumphs of a former governor of the Company, John
Churchill, Duke of Marlborough, should have made recovery possible.

But the Treaty of Utrecht not only restored the Bay, it also acknowledged the cession of Acadia. In 1710, for the third time, Port Royal succumbed to New England militiamen, and the change of the name to Annapolis Royal, in honour of Queen Anne, was final. Yet the British were to give little attention to their new province of Nova Scotia; not until 1749 was Halifax established as a port and focus of maritime settlement. From Halifax, British patrols could keep an eye on Cape Breton Island, where fortress Louisbourg stood sentinel, guarding the mouth of the St Lawrence and the way to Quebec.

In 1710 the English occupied the early French settlement Port-Royal (Nova Scotia), and renamed it Annapolis Royal. A view of 1751 (*below*) and the fort today (*right*).

Meanwhile, at home, French administration was beginning to show signs of the disorder and decay that were eventually to lead to revolution; yet imperial ambitions remained as sublime as in the halcyon days of the Grand Monarch. Indeed, French policy in North America seemed to be spurred by an almost feverish aggressiveness, as soldiers and traders continued their efforts to prevent the expanding British colonies from trespassing on the fur-bearing regions south of the Great Lakes. In 1726 Niagara was built to keep watch on the threatening British post at Oswego on the south-east shore of Lake Ontario; Detroit was established to guard the approaches to Lake Huron, while the Ohio country was reinforced by forts on the Wabash and Illinois. Eventually, the chain of military posts was extended westwards north of Lake Superior as far as the Saskatchewan River, in an effort to exploit new hunting-grounds against the competition of British traders operating from Hudson Bay.

In 1731-2 Pierre Gaultier de la Vérendrye struggled across the desolate escarpment of the Great Shield as far as Lake of the Woods, where he established Fort Charles; two years later a second post was built on the banks of the Red River. With expert *voyageurs* and by skilful native diplomacy the French were gradually linking their Montreal headquarters with the far west. Apart from physical force there was no other way of combating British competition from the Bay. But the process of pushing the frontier westward was expensive. The increased returns from furs scarcely balanced the additional costs imposed by military and transport needs. Muskets, ammunition, kettles and other forms of hardware on which the Indian was now dependent could obviously be supplied much more cheaply from Hudson Bay than from Montreal. Even the wear and tear on moccasins over the long portages was an item of significance which could not be ignored in adding up the overheads.

None the less, such enveloping tactics gave the French an immediate strategic initiative in the event of war. At the same time, Canada was well placed to resist any British effort to roll up the interior approaches to Montreal and Quebec. Direct access from the south could be achieved only along water routes – by Lake Champlain and the Richelieu River, or from the upper Ohio to Lake Ontario. These passages the French were confident they could block by means of forts, supported by well-trained

French professional troops drilling at Quebec.

professional troops. When the time of final struggle for supremacy arrived, France could only hope to fight a defensive war, holding or wearing down British and colonial forces until she could perchance reap the benefit of victories on the European continent.

Considered in this light, the French policy of concentrating on a strong field army was sensible. It was essential to play for time. A few successful land campaigns might well confuse and dishearten the enemy, and conceivably delay defeat until weary diplomats met round the peace table. In 1748 French ministers were to comfort themselves with the thought that their majestic fortress at Louisbourg, captured by a scratch force of New England militia in 1745, had been returned under the Treaty of Aix-la-Chapelle. Because Marshal Maurice de Saxe had been able to seize and hold the Low Countries, France bartered successfully for the return of her cherished North American outpost.

To counter Louisbourg (*below*), which commanded the entrance to the St Lawrence, the English founded a rival naval base at Halifax in 1749. It is shown at left with an English squadron proceeding to an attack on Louisbourg, which fell to Wolfe's forces in July 1758.

The War of the Austrian Succession was a preliminary trial of strength; the Treaty of Aix-la-Chapelle represented little more than an official truce before the conclusive testing. In North America scattered fighting on the frontier broke out as early as 1750; and Voltaire was amused that the shot which heralded a world war should have been fired in the backwoods of America. In 1753 French forces pushed southward from Lake Erie, and in the following year established a post at the junction of the Allegheny and Monongahela rivers (where the city of Pittsburgh now stands) which they named, after the Governor of Canada, Fort Duquesne. An outstanding young soldier and bush-ranger from Virginia, George Washington, was sent to destroy it. Following a brief encounter, Washington was obliged to surrender to superior forces. One year later, General Edward Braddock made his dramatic and disastrous march in the same direction. When official war was finally declared in Europe early in 1756, Fort Duquesne and the Ohio Valley were still in *Conquest* the hands of France. Not until William Pitt came to power in June of *of Canada* 1757 did the conquest of Canada become a prime objective of British strategy. 'England has been a long time in labour,' wrote Frederick of Prussia, 'but at last she has brought forth a man.'

But even Pitt looked at North America through European glasses. He was determined to destroy the maritime and colonial power of France, but this grim decision must not be interpreted as a desire to place colonial ahead of European considerations. His plan to conquer Canada was part of a larger strategy that he had long pondered. By assaulting French possessions all over the world and eliminating French overseas commerce, Pitt counted on destroying France in Europe. To safeguard Britain, he intended to demolish French maritime power and the colonies which depended for their existence upon it. By adding to British territory and commerce at the expense of France, Britain would have the necessary strength to maintain the European balance so essential to her security.

Pitt's strategy of conquest, thanks to the efficient performance of Frederick on the Continent, was based on the use of overwhelming power by land and sea. French troops and supply ships were to be kept bottled up in Toulon, Rochefort and Brest, while British and colonial

William Pitt,
Earl of Chatham.

troops swept up the French defences in the course of a triple-pronged advance: in the Ohio country against Fort Duquesne, and thence to the St Lawrence Valley by way of Forts Niagara and Frontenac (Kingston); in the centre, up the Lake Champlain route, where Crown Point and Ticonderoga guarded the way to Montreal; and in the east, after occupying or neutralizing Louisbourg, up the St Lawrence River to Quebec. During the summer of 1758 the great machine began to roll slowly but relentlessly. In the west, Forts Duquesne and Niagara fell, and the loss of the upper Ohio broke the links that once had tied Louisiana to Canada. Brigadier John Forbes won no major battles and no fame, but his successes opened the West to English enterprise. In the centre, however, Abercromby's costly defeat at Ticonderoga upset Pitt's time-table, and the subsequent progress of General Jeffrey Amherst by the Lake Champlain route to Montreal was painfully slow. Consequently the main blow had to be struck on the eastern flank from the sea.

The collapse of Louisbourg's tawdry masonry in July 1758, by removing a potential threat to British communications, opened the way to Quebec. The amphibious operations culminating on the Plains of Abraham in September 1759 with the death of Wolfe and the gallant Marquis de Montcalm, did not mean the conquest of Canada. At the end of the winter General James Murray's half-famished and

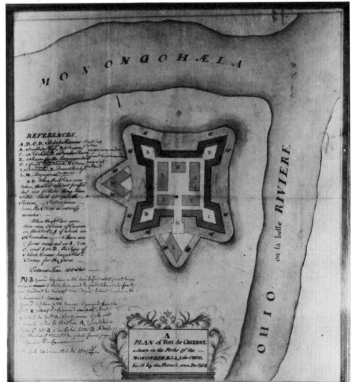

Plan of Fort Duquesne (site of Pittsburgh) drawn by a Scots soldier who was imprisoned there by the French in 1751.

James Wolfe,
drawn during the siege of Quebec.

Chevalier de Lévis.

Louis Joseph,
Marquis de Montcalm in 1759.

FRANÇOIS GASTON DE LÉVIS BRIGADIER des ARMÉES du ROI de FRANCE
AU CANADA puis MARÉCHAL DE FRANCE, DUC de LÉVIS, CHEVALIER
DES ORDRES DU ROI GOUVERNEUR de la PROVINCE D'ARTOIS NÉ EN
1720 MORT EN 1787

Wolfe's victory on the Plains of Abraham before Quebec.

scurvy-ridden garrison were, in their turn, besieged by French forces from Montreal under the Chevalier de Lévis, and only the timely arrival of a relief squadron in May 1760 prevented their surrender. Montcalm's death had come close to being avenged. By September Murray was able to join forces with Amherst before Montreal, and the capitulation of its stubborn defenders sealed the end of New France. Under the terms of the Peace of Paris, 10 February 1763, Britain took over the whole continent east of the Mississippi, except the town of New Orleans which was ceded by France to Spain. Of her former empire, France kept only the two little islands of St Pierre and Miquelon, off the south coast of Newfoundland.

93

General James Murray,
the first British
Governor of Canada.

For the moment, French Canada seemed to face not only political but social and cultural annihilation at the hands of the hereditary enemy. Generations of savage frontier strife had left a legacy of bitterness that the most charitable intentions on the part of the conqueror seemed unlikely to assuage. That New France did survive the conquest owed nothing to historical ties with the mother country. Most of the adminis-trative officers and the educated bourgeoisie had returned to France, leaving the rest of the population to the mercies of the dreaded *Bastonnais*. Fortunately, few of the lower clergy accompanied them, and almost overnight the Church became the refuge and rallying-point for a deserted people. In the years ahead, it was to the parish priest that the stricken *habitant* entrusted not only his soul but his destinies.

But how would the conqueror respond to this unique situation? Although Britain was dealing with a race of equal civilization to her own, it was one whose traditions and religion were anathema to her. In England, no Roman Catholic could hold public office or be an officer in the army or navy; in French Canada, as a result of the ban on Huguenot emigration, Protestants were almost as rare as Negroes. Inheriting through the missionaries the pure milk of the seventeenth-century Catholic reformation, colonial Catholicism had become abso-lute and fixed in its unquestioned conservatism. When Old France a few years later succumbed to the virus of revolutionary principles, *le canadien*, quite unaware of the Rights of Man, remained unaffected. If anything, the French Revolution was to deepen the gulf between New France and Old, which the conquest of 1760 had opened.

In these circumstances, it was fortunate that the colony remained for almost four years under the rule of military governors, who very sensibly made no effort to change the French Canadian mentality and way of life. They neither spurned nor condemned without discrimination habits of mind and customs that they knew little or nothing about. Indeed, they regarded much of the British code they were expected to enforce as largely inapplicable because it was based on alien conceptions and usages. And when General James Murray, in August 1764, became the first head of civil government in the newly created province of Quebec, he promptly shelved the notion of a legislative assembly as unfitted to a community whose Catholic electorate, under the laws of England, would have been at the mercy of a minority of Protestant merchants.

Similarly, he and his successor, Governor Guy Carleton, insisted that the French Canadian should be protected in his ancient laws and customs, especially in matters relating to land tenure, and both sup-ported the use of French civil law in the courts. Gradually, however, as certain benefits of English commercial law became known, a curious hybrid of French custom and English law developed. This nascent Common Law was not always intelligible to either judges or advocates, but it appears to have been accepted as a beneficial compromise. Cer-tainly any attempt to replace French customary law by English civil law would have been disastrous. An old French colony could not with the stroke of a pen be forced into the same pattern as the Thirteen Colonies

Governor
Guy Carleton.

The Anglican Cathedral of St Paul, Halifax, in 1749.

to the south. To have tried to coerce the *habitant*, as the incoming British merchants from Boston and New York wished, into the British parliamentary mould would have been to court disaster.

Quebec Act of 1774　　Such was certainly the attitude which influenced the British government, when, in 1774, they passed the Quebec Act. Indeed, because of threatening war clouds to the south, they bent over backwards in an effort to keep a contented colony within the Empire. The old French civil law was restored in its entirety, although the Crown reserved the right to grant lands according to English freehold tenure. English criminal law, presumably milder than the French equivalent, was introduced and doubtless welcomed. Freedom to practise the Roman Catholic religion was re-emphasized, and the clergy were allowed to enforce payment of their accustomed dues, especially the tithe. And since the province had little experience in the art of representative government the Act made no provision for an assembly. Government was entrusted to a governor and a council composed of not fewer than seventeen or more than twenty-three members appointed by the Crown – in fact, chosen by the governor.

The Catholic Notre-Dame de Bonsecours, built in 1776 in Montreal.

Although some such measure was necessary to clear up the confusion in regard to laws and religion, the Quebec Act was also an act of expediency to preserve Canada at a time when murmurs of rebellion to the southward seemed likely to threaten the stability of British rule in North America. As such, it failed in its purpose. The *habitants*, while turning a deaf ear to the seductive invitations of the Americans, were equally reluctant to enlist in the British cause. The vast majority of French Canadians refused to have anything to do with the war; fewer than four hundred fought on the Loyalist side; only a handful joined the rebels. On the other hand, the clergy and seigneurs, while preserving a respectable neutrality, gave their sympathy to their recent conquerors. The clauses which had finally settled the status of the Roman Catholic Church (by granting emancipation half a century before it was achieved in Britain) won the loyalty of most of the priests; the legal provisions which prescribed French civil law were not unappreciated by the seigneurs.

Unfortunately, Governor Carleton, who was responsible for implementing the Act, failed to carry out supplementary instructions, which might have diluted the natural resentments of the English merchant class. Fearful of offending French Canadian feelings at a time when invasion threatened from the south, and convinced that, barring catastrophe, Canada 'must to the end of time be peopled by the Canadian race', he left the merchant minority for ten years without the benefits of *habeas corpus*, trial by jury in civil cases, and some of the safeguards provided by English commercial law which they had enjoyed since 1764.

American invading forces led by Richard Montgomery and Benedict Arnold tried to capture Quebec in 1775. The assault on the night of 31 December 1775 (*left*) was repulsed, and General Montgomery was killed.

At the end of the War of Independence, thousands of Loyalists migrated from the new United States to Canada and the British Atlantic provinces. *Above*, a typical Loyalist settlement in the province of New Brunswick, which was created in 1784.

Although the boundary clause, which extended the colony's limits southward between the Mississippi and Ohio rivers, was regarded by many Americans as a Machiavellian British effort to block their westward expansion, the Quebec Act scarcely affected the course of events leading to bloodshed and war. On the other hand, the war for independence deeply affected the purposes of the Quebec Act. As a consequence of British military failures, thousands of Loyalists migrated voluntarily or were subsequently hustled into Canada and the Maritime provinces. The thirty thousand or more who took refuge in Nova Scotia, Cape Breton, New Brunswick and Prince Edward Island created no problem. From the first they had enjoyed traditional colonial self-government, and with the exception of Cape Breton had practised

American Loyalist Immigration

it through the medium of elected assemblies. But a thousand miles to the west, the situation was fraught with difficulty and danger.

Most of the seven thousand Loyalists who crossed into the St Lawrence Valley had been nursed in the ethos of self-governing institutions, and they were bound to resent the restrictive bonds of a constitutional system established to pacify and meet the needs of a politically immature population. On the other hand, French Canadians

were bound to be disturbed by an invasion of fiercely British immigrants, who were certain to demand their accustomed liberties. Fearful of losing their recently guaranteed religion, language and institutions, they impulsively sought refuge within the legal walls of the Quebec Act, transforming what had been intended by the British government as a temporary 'halting-ground' into a privileged sanctuary. In this sense, the American Revolution was responsible, not only for imposing

Newly arrived Loyalists camping at Johnston on the St Lawrence, near the present-day town of Prescott, Ontario (1784).

on Canada a racial duality, but for consolidating a new and un-
compromising spirit of race nationalism.

Constitutional   An earnest attempt to find a solution was made in 1791. The
Act of 1791   Constitutional Act of that year provided for the grant of elective
legislative assemblies within two distinct provinces separated by the
Ottawa River: Upper Canada in the west, and Lower Canada in the
east. 'New France' of the Old Régime could continue to live its own life,
but under a parliamentary system of government as democratic as any
then practised in the world outside the United States. For the moment,
however, French Canadians ignored the strange apparatus which had
been thrust upon them, and which actually bolstered their position
against potential domination by the English-speaking settlers. Not until
the lapse of a decade and more did members of the assembly of Lower
Canada learn to regard themselves as a permanent Opposition, whose
principal object was to preserve *la nation canadienne*. This was to be
accomplished by waging constant war against the authority and independence of a British executive that commanded the patronage of
government, membership of the legislative council and the better-paid
jobs in administration.

The classic duel between governor and assembly, which had
dominated the later political history of the Thirteen Colonies, was about
to be repeated. Constitutional issues such as the control of revenue and
taxing power were to be bitterly contested in both provinces. Yet deep
down, the French Canadian was not interested in democratic procedure; he scorned the methods and institutions of his conqueror
because they were the works of an intruder. He was concerned not with
the principle of reform for its own sake, but with the practical use of
the elected assembly as an instrument for the exploitation of grievances
and the promotion of race nationalism.

During the long Napoleonic Wars which followed the outbreak of the
French Revolution, British possessions in North America were never
in danger of invasion so long as Britain kept command of the sea and
the United States remained neutral. Secret agents occasionally reported
treasonous plots and suspected tamperings with the loyalty of British
Indians, but the official correspondence contains few direct references
to the titanic struggle that was racking Europe. People submerged in
tasks of pioneer settlement lived in a world of their own. Aloof from
the main stream of events that settled the fate of empires, they were
content to ignore the war, unless called upon by government to celebrate
a victory of 'the Nile' or a 'Cape St Vincent'. Apart from occasional
cargoes of masts and a little wheat, there were not many local products
to sell to the beleaguered mother country. Not until after 1809 did the
colonies profit from the collaboration of Napoleon and Alexander of
Russia, a brief alliance which, by blocking British sources in the
Baltic, forced the spectacular rise of the Canadian timber trade.

Now and then small supplies of flour, grain, cod-fish, lumber or
barrel-hoops found their way to the West Indies, but generally the
settlers found themselves hard-pressed to provide for their own bodily
needs. The great majority of the Loyalists in Upper Canada were still
subsistence farmers; the *habitants* rarely eked out surpluses from the

103

Lumbermen on the Miramichi River in the early nineteenth century.

The isolated farm of a settler: Bush Farm near Chatham, Upper Canada, c. 1838.

Horace-Ville, on the Ottawa River, was one of many small communities built along river-banks.

narrow strips which bordered the St Lawrence, and the newcomers to Nova Scotia and New Brunswick had become increasingly dependent on the United States for bread, flour and other provisions. Even the Maritimes' fisheries were to suffer in competition with the more efficient and subsidized industry of New England. Until American embargoes, which ushered in the War of 1812, stimulated a clandestine trade over the borders, the British provinces stayed relatively undeveloped and inert.

The absence of other than the most primitive transportation facilities did not encourage the growth of towns and local markets. Distances between villages were long, and roads non-existent or exceedingly rough and treacherous, apart from the river highways which in winter could be used by sleighs. Almost all immigrants who entered Upper Canada from the east travelled up the St Lawrence in the narrow *bateau*; after 1809, the larger, flat-bottomed Durham boat was

Transportation

introduced. But rapids, less turbulent than the notorious Lachine, compelled awkward portages, and communication with the Upper Lakes was not possible until 1830, when the first Welland Canal provided a detour round Niagara Falls. The first lieutenant-governor of Upper Canada, Colonel John Graves Simcoe was responsible for the first major road-building operations; these comprised highways from York (Toronto), which had become the capital in 1797, to Lake Simcoe, and from Toronto to Montreal. The latter proved to be a difficult project, and it was not completed until after the War of 1812; by that time the stage-coach had replaced the one-horse post-chaise. Nevertheless, pioneer travel remained slow and uncomfortable, until John Macadam's

Stage-coaches were equipped with runners to cross the snow as sleighs (*below*), and passage through the forests was often halted by fallen trees (*right*).

unique stone and gravel surface process accomplished for land traffic what the Quebec-built *Royal William* and her steam successors achieved on the sea. By 1840, Samuel Cunard's steamship company was able to link Liverpool with his home town, Halifax, in fourteen days.

Meanwhile, American farmers and speculators had been trickling over the unguarded frontier into Upper Canada in search of cheaper land or bigger profits. By 1812 probably no more than one-fifth of the population was British; another fifth may have been genuine Loyalist, but at least three-fifths were non-Loyalist colonists from the United States. Inevitably many of these recent immigrants were tempted by the vision of their adopted country as a future territory of the Republic, and this predilection was reinforced by the greed of the American frontiersman, pushing relentlessly westward beyond the Ohio in the

Flat-bottomed Durham boats were used on the St Lawrence River.

An Indian of our own times portaging a canoe.

108

The Governor of Red River, a Hudson's Bay Company settlement on the edge of the Western prairies, in a light canoe (1824).

The introduction of steam revolutionized travel in eastern Canada. The *Royal William*, built in 1831, linked Quebec and Halifax; in 1833 it was the first vessel to cross the Atlantic using steam as its main source of power.

direction of the Mississippi. To this fur-producing homeland, vacated slowly and reluctantly by established Canadian traders, the Indian hunters and trappers clung obstinately. The result was sporadic warfare, as the Indians fought back desperately with the guns and ammunition supplied by their allies and partners in exchange for furs. In the view of the angry frontiersman the only way to secure the western region for civilization and settlement was to eradicate the Canadian fur trader, a proceeding which could be most effectively accomplished by acquiring his base of operations in Canada.

American
Designs on
Canada

'I believe that in four weeks from the time a declaration of war is heard on our frontier,' cried John C. Calhoun, one of the leaders of the War Hawks, 'the whole of Upper Canada and a part of Lower Canada will be in our power.' To many impetuous politicians like Henry Clay the Canadas represented an ugly blotch on the North American continent, the site of an unwholesome monarchical government which should soon be cleansed with the help of their fellow-countrymen already resident in the country. Young Americans, declared a future President, Andrew Jackson, 'will never prefer an inglorious sloth, a supine activity to the honorable toil of carrying the Republican standard to the Heights of Abraham'.

As it happened, the designs of the western expansionists were being steadily promoted at sea by the activity of the Royal Navy. British maritime policy towards neutrals was rousing increasing resentment in the United States. In the fight for survival that began in 1793, Britain was bound in self-interest to deal severely, if not unscrupulously, with any non-belligerent power whose trade routes crossed the Atlantic to

A medal of 1813 proclaiming the successful defence of Upper Canada against the United States. An American eagle looks across the Niagara river towards a Canadian beaver and British lion.

The United States frigate *Chesapeake* being brought into Halifax harbour, 1807.

continental Europe. The crisis came in 1807 when British Orders-in-Council practically closed Napoleon's Europe to neutral commerce. These Orders were the obvious answer to Napoleon's Berlin Decree which had imposed in the previous year an unenforcible blockade of the British Isles. But Britain also insisted on the right of searching American vessels for deserters, and British captains, dangerously short of crews, were not always scrupulous in identifying those of true British nationality.

In time of war, international rules for determining the rights of neutrals and belligerents have never sufficed to meet the demands of either, once an issue has arisen. In June 1807 the two nations were brought to the brink of hostilities as the result of an encounter between HMS *Leopard* and the United States' frigate *Chesapeake*. The American press fulminated, and the young officer who fired a lone gun with a live coal in his fingers became a national hero. It was this incident which impelled the American government to more aggressive action, leading to retributive embargoes and ultimately, in June 1812, to a declaration of war.

The War of 1812. Major-General Sir Isaac Brock (*below*) was killed at the Battle of Queenston Heights near Niagara in October 1812 (*right*).

War of 1812   On the ocean American seamen were to show infinite courage and resource, but single ship actions could scarcely affect Britain's command of the seas. The significant, indeed crucial, feature of the war was the American effort to conquer Canada by land. It was an enterprise which on paper seemed certain to succeed. The total population of British North America was probably 500,000, of which barely 80,000 lived in Upper Canada. The number of regular troops available to defend the inland frontier of a thousand miles was less than 5,000, of which less than half, under the command of General Isaac Brock, were stationed in the vulnerable upper province, where the invasion was clearly intended to begin.

The American standing army was not much larger than the British, but out of a population of more than six millions, the United States, before the end of the war, was able to put nearly half a million men in the field. Admittedly, the majority were poorly trained and lacked competent leadership, but it was optimistically assumed that any weaknesses in morale or efficiency would be compensated by aid from nostalgic immigrants (assumed to be nearly a third of the Canadian population) and discontented *habitants*. Indeed, the early campaigns were advertised as crusades of emancipation; the oppressed and the aggrieved were invited to throw off the monarchical yoke and join the Union of the free.

In September 1813 the Americans under Commodore Oliver Perry gained control of Lake Erie following the defeat of Captain Robert Barclay at Put-in-Bay.

In the event, the acquisition of Canada proved to be more than 'a mere matter of marching', as Thomas Jefferson had incautiously suggested. Owing to New England's opposition to the war, the potential strength of the United States was never fully exerted. Moreover, the danger of intervention by American sympathizers was reduced by General Brock's declaration of martial law, and eventually eliminated by the enthusiasm of Loyalists thirsting to avenge their wrongs. The reaction of the French Canadians, as might have been expected, was tepid; few joined the local militia; but even fewer joined the enemy. Although the American navy won control of Lake Erie, the invading armies effected no permanent breach in the Canadian frontier, and while it would be an exaggeration to suggest that this triumphant resistance generated a Canadian national sentiment – British regulars bore the brunt of the fighting – undoubtedly some seeds of common feeling took tenuous root. Indeed, for a brief moment it seemed possible that common sufferings and mutual fears of conquest might breed a new concept of national loyalty, transcending race and politics.

The inconclusive Treaty of Ghent ended an inconclusive war in December 1814. In the course of the negotiations, the plenipotentiaries of both countries withdrew impossible claims, and in general accepted a return of the *status quo ante bellum*. No mention was made of Orders-in-

Council or the right of search. Both sides showed an anxiety to wipe out the past – the first significant hint of a new approach to Anglo-American relations – and within four years were able to arrange an agreement for the limitation of armaments of the Great Lakes, settle the tangled inshore fisheries question and establish Canada's southern boundary along the forty-ninth parallel from Lake of the Woods to the Rocky Mountains. Not until 1846 did the Oregon Treaty extend this line westward to the Pacific Ocean, where it was allowed to dip southward to include Vancouver Island.

In 1815 all the British North American provinces – Upper and Lower Canada, Nova Scotia, New Brunswick, Prince Edward Island and Newfoundland – possessed the traditional colonial apparatus of administration. They had governors sent out by Britain, executive councils nominated by the governors, and representative assemblies with control of local legislation and taxation. But like the elected bodies in the erstwhile American colonies, the Canadian assemblies resented the limitations on their powers, and used whatever limited authority they possessed to make efficient government difficult, if not impossible. In the Atlantic provinces friction never reached serious proportions, but in Upper Canada the ineptness and conceit of the Establishment, known as the Family Compact, was bound to encourage the kind of virulent opposition that so often leads to violence. In Lower Canada, the same situation was exacerbated by bitter racial conflict. The execu- *Racial* tive was entirely British, the assembly almost entirely French; a head-on *Conflict* collision was sooner or later inevitable.

But whether or not the future course of Canadian domestic politics was to be marked by the spirit of co-operation, one thing at least seemed clear: reform whenever it came would follow British rather than American precedent. Although the war did little, in the long run, to forge any sort of Canadian national consciousness, it did confirm the country in its British connection, while sharpening the antagonism of the governing classes for the United States. Americans of strong republican sentiments had withdrawn or been driven out; those who remained pledged their allegiance to the Crown.

A Pickwickian-style election at Perth, Upper Canada, 1828.

On the other hand, although the process of Americanization by immigration had been checked, in Upper Canada religious bodies like the Methodists, with close affiliations south of the border, helped to preserve much of the American ethos. Inevitably, leaders of the radical party like William Lyon Mackenzie were encouraged to seek the support of such democratic elements by appealing to the spirit of the American Revolution. In reaction to the government's attempt to establish oligarchical rule by a privileged social class and a privileged Anglican Church, they attacked the British representative system and demanded government on the American model with its predominantly elective institutions.

In fact, nothing did more to retard the growth of a healthy radicalism in Canada than this embittered use of the American example. Advocacy

The Woolsey family, merchants of Lower Canada, were examples of what was called the British privileged class.

of the American concept of democracy, rather than encouraging the growth of Canadian self-government, actually impeded it. The struggle for responsible government in the Canadas was almost as much a battle against Canadian conservatives and moderates who loathed the egalitarian aspects of American political life, as it was a struggle against traditional authority represented by an over-cautious and imperious mother country. Supporters of the British parliamentary system never equated popular democracy with liberty; they inclined to put their emphasis on individual liberty under the law. And it was the *rule of law* that above all else was to shape future Canadian concepts of democracy. This urge to cultivate British parliamentary procedure was not necessarily based on any full comprehension of British practice but it was deeply influenced by a distrust of and disdain for republican models.

Rebellion   In Lower Canada the War of 1812 did temporarily, as has been noticed, assuage political strife, but within a few years the agitation for constitutional reform became, in the hands of extremists like Louis-Joseph Papineau, the cloak for a campaign of race nationalism. Whereas the Upper Canada assembly, in return for increased taxing authority, agreed in 1831 to provide a permanent civil list, the French assembly was intransigent. In short, their so-called reform movement was primarily an expression of their determination to control their own destinies as a cultural entity: '*Soyons nous même.*' The leaders of the assembly sought control of the executive as a means of protecting the French Canadian way of life against the advancing tide of merchant influence as represented by land settlement companies, registry offices,

LE CANADIEN

NOS INSTITUTIONS, NOTRE LANGUE ET NOS LOIS

Le Canadien, a French-language newspaper, was used by Louis-Joseph Papineau (*left*) as the organ of the French-Canadian reform party.

William Lyon Mackenzie attempted in 1837 to incite radical rebellion in Toronto. After its failure he and some of his followers fled to Navy Island in the Niagara River, where they organized a Patriotic force. *Below*, Navy Island money issued to one of Mackenzie's supporters on the security of a successful *coup d'état*.

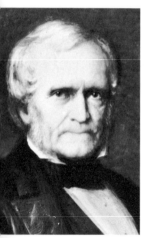

$10. Provisional Government of Upper Canada. No. 867

Navy Island, Upper Canada, December 27, 1837. Four months after date, the Provisional Government of Upper Canada, promise to pay to *John Rolph* or order, at the City Hall, Toronto, Ten Dollars, for value received. (*Ten Dollars.*)

Entered by the Secretary,

S. Parson   *W. L. Mackenzie*
                Chairman pro. tem. Ex. Com.

Examined by the Comptroller,

David Gibson   ($10:)

immigration boards and various agencies for initiating internal improvements.

The Canadian uprising of 1837 was not a real rebellion; only a handful of the population participated, and in neither province did it reach dangerous proportions. In Upper Canada it could have been avoided had not the lieutenant governor, Sir Francis Bond Head, deliberately withdrawn his troops from the scene of trouble in order that the small refractory minority should play into his hands. In Lower Canada a few perfunctory outbreaks of violence were the work of discontented extremists. The Roman Catholic Church refused from the beginning to support them and this decisive stand on the part of the clergy made failure inevitable.

Yet the rebellion was sufficiently serious, or at least unexpected, to induce the British government to suspend the government of Lower Canada, and to re-examine the whole question of colonial government *vis à vis* the supreme authority in Westminster. British political opinion had changed radically since 1791 when faith in traditional institutions had led to the Canada Act, and more stringent control from the imperial centre. During the first three decades of the nineteenth century, Church and State, Navigation System and Corn Laws had been subject

Sir Francis Bond Head.

The American steam packet *Caroline*, which ferried supplies to Mackenzie's camp on Navy Island, was 'cut out' in American waters, and sent in flames towards Niagara Falls.

119

Repulse of the rebels
in 1838,
at Dickinson's Landing
(now submerged by the
St Lawrence Seaway),
8 miles west of Cornwall.
This operation was linked
with an attempted invasion
of Lower Canada
by *patriotes* who had fled
to Vermont in 1837.

to continuous assault on the part of men who believed in cutting industrial England free from the dead weight of custom. A new middle class, infected by the profit motive, and dominated by the impulsions of the factory age, was unable to accept sacrosanct traditions of government that had moulded the attitudes of the old governing classes. With an eye to immediate advantage, and bitterly critical of all institutions or laws which might hamper their own progress, they began to demand a free field for the Industrial Revolution.

This withering challenge to stereotyped orthodoxy, voiced by men like Jeremy Bentham and William Huskisson, paved the way for the Great Reform Bill of 1832 – a Bill which by recognizing the existence of a previously unenfranchised class substantially altered the spirit of English society. Such a revolution had, as its inevitable corollary, the reform of colonial institutions and imperial practices. Because an intractable problem had been precipitated by a minor rebellion, Canada was to become the classic example of an experiment in self-government.

Although the man whom the British government sent out to investigate the disturbances had little connection with the Whig Establishment (he was known as 'Radical Jack'), Lord Durham was almost bound to align himself with the English-speaking people. He had an honest sympathy for French Canadians as individuals, but he was incapable of appreciating their fears of Anglo-Saxon domination, and their determination to live, even in isolation, as a separate entity. He recognized that the Lower Canada rebellion was essentially a racial conflict – 'two nations warring within the bosom of a single state' – but like the elder Pitt, his own imperialism allowed for no diversity of nationality. His advanced liberal approach to English politics in no way affected his assumption that only a homogeneous state could survive in peace and unity. For him there was only one solution to the problem of racial conflict; French Canada must be submerged, and he counted on increased British immigration to tilt the balance until the French population should have been thoroughly assimilated. The result was a union of the two Canadas in 1840 under a single government.

Underestimating the tenacity of the *habitant*, as well as his fertility (later symbolized by the slogan '*La revanche des berceaux*'), Durham's scheme of amalgamation was as unworkable as it was unwise. His vision of a British North American nationality based on the complete political and cultural ascendancy of a British population had no chance of realization. French Canadian language and customs could be neither extinguished nor diluted.

Robert Baldwin.

Nevertheless, although his analysis of the racial problem was inaccurate and partisan, his less exciting recommendation has stood the test of time. Local interests, he wrote in his Report, were obviously as important to the colonists as were imperial interests to the mother country. In his opinion it was absurd, on matters of purely domestic concern, to depend on the advice and decisions of a government three thousand miles across the ocean. To break the chronic deadlock between executive and elected assembly he simply recommended that the executive or cabinet should be made responsible to the majority of the elected assembly in every matter relating to local affairs. Major

AFFECTING INTERVIEW between LORD D_____M and the CANADIAN DELEGATES.
AT QUEBEC, ON THE 22ᵗ OF SEPTᵗ 1838.

Cartoon on Lord Durham's resignation, five months after his arrival in Canada.

problems such as foreign affairs, the form of government, external trade and the disposal of Crown lands could be left with the Crown.

Responsible government in local affairs was scarcely a new concept. During the decade before the Rebellion, prescient Canadians like Dr William Baldwin and his son Robert had been mulling over ways and means of side-tracking radical proposals for a constitution on the American model. Although no firm solution crystallized, Durham's outright demand that a reorganized Empire should advance on the

123

Lord Elgin.

basis of self-government for the parts was the obvious response to a long-standing dilemma. However incidental to the main substance of the Report, this proved to be the most enduring of his recommendations. By laying the ground for evolutionary processes to develop within the colonial body politic Durham had provided the alternative to revolution.

None the less, the shock to British Cabinet ministers is understandable. Tories like Wellington and Whigs like Lord John Russell recoiled in dismay before the prospect. To whom, they asked, is the colonial governor to be responsible? If to the British government, then he cannot be responsible to his colonial ministers; if to his colonial ministers, then you are faced with an independent state. A colony threatened from without by a powerful and aggressive neighbour and from within by deep racial cleavages required, in their view, the utmost in centralized and protective administration, if it were to continue to exist.

Consequently during the next few years, British ministers moved cautiously. Between 1840 and 1846 the Melbourne and Peel administrations did their best to maintain the responsibility of the executive to the home authorities without too obviously treading on the privileges and feelings of the elected assemblies. It was a salutary period of marking time; the arts of political leadership could not be learned in a day. But the granting of the full measure of responsible government could not long be postponed. By 1847 it had been conceded in Nova Scotia and New Brunswick; in 1849, by assenting to a bad Bill on the grounds that it had the support of the elected majority, the Governor of United Canada, Lord Elgin, set the seal on Durham's promise of self-government. An issue that had daunted wise men like Pitt and Burke before the American Revolution had been finally settled, and so decisively as to provide a formula of constitutional evolution for other parts of the Empire. By 1855 the same system of responsible government had been introduced into Australia and New Zealand.

With Europe's problems pressing heavily upon their shoulders, British statesmen naturally hoped that the amalgamation of Upper and Lower Canada into the united province of Canada would see the end of racial and political disorders. They were soon to be disillusioned. The Durham proposal of assimilation was abandoned, but the mere suggestion of cultural extinction had deeply bruised a sensitive people, who looked with renewed suspicion on their dominating English partner across the Ottawa River. At the time of the Act of Union (1840) the former

Act of Union, 1840

British Canadian opposition to Lord Elgin's Rebellion Losses Bill which offered compensation to French Canadians for property damaged during the 1837 rebellion.

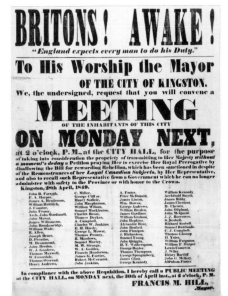

Lower Canada had a population of some 600,000 compared with 450,000 in the upper province. But British immigration had steadily reversed the balance; by 1861, the English-speaking section, with a population of about 1,400,000, outnumbered the French-speaking section by at least 60,000.

In the beginning there had been a tacit understanding that French and English domestic issues would not be decided in the assembly against hostile majorities representing the section affected. For example, it was intended that legislation involving land, revenue or law east of the Ottawa River, should be settled by the French-speaking members, without the intervention of the English. This awkward system, which often involved the use of double majorities, worked spasmodically for a time thanks to the skill of moderate leaders on both sides. But the strains that developed in the process made anything like efficient administration impossible. In the circumstances, the demand for 'representation by population' on the part of English-speaking back-benchers merely served to augment the chronic racial cleavage and reduce self-government to a farce. By 1864 Parliament had ceased to function; the assembly had reached a stage of complete deadlock, which two general elections failed to break. The union which Lord Durham had projected was doomed. The only hope seemed to lie in dissolving the partnership, and perhaps re-establishing the separated pair as members of a wider combination to include the whole of British North America.

Durham had pondered this bold concept during his visit, and admitted that a federal arrangement would in theory provide the ideal solution. But in the absence of communications – even decent roads – to bridge the gulf between the Maritimes and the settlements on the Pacific coast, it appeared to him quite impracticable. A union of the Maritime provinces was sensible, but a federation that would include the vast almost untenanted Hudson Bay territories in the west and north-west was something to contemplate in the distant future. A common British sentiment could scarcely subdue the wilderness of the Great Shield and the colossal barrier of mountains that separated eight hundred miles of prairie from the Pacific mainland.

Although the first forty years after Waterloo saw the longest peaceful interlude in the modern history of the Western world, war remained the blunt but decisive instrument of statecraft. After the Treaty of Ghent which concluded the first and only Anglo-American war in 1814, political observers, both British and American, confidently assumed that only another armed contest could settle all the outstanding controversies. As late as 1838 James Buchanan, the British Consul in New York, warned his government that war could be anticipated on fifteen different grounds, and that all these potential causes of war had been brewing for fifteen years.

British statesmen retained serious doubts as to the commercial value of their vulnerable and expensive possessions, but they were never prepared to abandon them to the mercies of hungry republicans without at least the show of a struggle. In their most despairing moments, they never considered giving them away, or trading them as part of a real estate deal. Apart from humanitarian considerations, prestige remained, as today, an important constituent of power; its loss or diminution was identical with 'loss of face'. Unfortunately, not many of the half million inhabitants of British North America were familiar with this reasoning. Most of them doubtless agreed with Lord Ashburton that Canada at least was 'the lamb awaiting the inevitable slaughter'. The United

Fear of the United States

127

The Citadel of Quebec, showing fortifications being rebuilt after the War of 1812, as part of the general defence against possible American attacks.

Empire Loyalists, the refugees of the American Revolution, quite naturally feared as well as hated their former persecutors. The oldest inhabitants, the French Canadians, had developed little affection for British institutions. They were 'non-aligned'; yet, as conservative Catholics, they were bound to view their republican neighbour with apprehension, if not abhorrence. Certainly, if war came, Canada would be once more invaded, and French Canadians saw little chance of preserving their cultural and religious safeguards should they cease to be British subjects.

In Britain intelligent soldiers realized that the inland provinces were not defensible; indeed, that flattering cliché of the future – 'three thousand miles of unguarded frontier' – may be ascribed solely to the

The Rideau Canal, built between 1826 and 1832, to link Lake Ontario with the Ottawa River, was planned as an alternative military route to the St Lawrence.

fact that Britain was in a position neither to build costly fortifications over so far flung a frontier, nor to defend them against the United States even if they had been built. None the less, a futile attempt to block the main gateways was made. Forts were built at Quebec and Kingston, and military canals like the Rideau and the Lachine were constructed at enormous expense. The British government spent millions against the probability of another war, and such token defences continued to be erected until 1871.

As for the United States, with superior manpower, good internal communications and a far more mature industrial organization than Canada, she could afford to neglect her northern frontier. History had taught Americans how easily the Royal Navy could bring its force to

Kingston, commanding communications between Montreal and Lake Ontario, was an important fortified town.

bear on their cities and trade routes from such convenient ports as Halifax and Bermuda. Hence, the Americans spent their millions in fortifying the Atlantic coastline. Only a fraction of the total for fixed defences was spent on the Canadian border.

Actually, because neither Britain nor the United States was anxious in the last resort to precipitate hostilities, friction never got beyond the stage of 'cold war'. In the 1840s when disputes over boundaries and slave extradition threatened to bring relations to the flash-point, Britain's foreign secretary, Lord Aberdeen, was quick to play his favourite role of peace-maker, and the American State Department was not ungrateful. Buttressing the mediators was 'big business', whose thriving free trade philosophy envisaged an abundance of accessible markets in a peaceful world. Wars were expensive, and especially wars to retain unprofitable colonies which sooner or later were likely to seek their independence.

American Civil War　Yet, at a time when friendly understanding between the two countries seemed to be more firmly established than ever before, the new-born harmony was to be broken by the American Civil War. During the first year of hostilities (1861), a large section of British public and official opinion supported the South, partly for sentimental reasons – at a distance the Southern plantation-owners looked like gentlemanly 'Cavaliers' – and partly no doubt because a divided Union would be a less forbidding rival and a less menacing colonial neighbour. Moreover, if the South should succeed in winning independence, it would undoubtedly open its ports to British goods on a free trade basis, and continue as formerly to supply the spindles of Lancashire with the necessary cotton. Whatever the motives British recognition of the Southern States as belligerents brought both governments to the brink of hostilities, and threatened to promote a second invasion of Canada. Scarcely more than four thousand regular troops were available to defend British North American frontiers. As a result of the policy of gradual withdrawal, the Canadian boundary was more vulnerable in 1864 than it had been in 1812.

The American Civil War. British artillerymen boarding ship at Liverpool to go to the defence of Canada.

After several years of frustration, American finance and British science combined to provide a permanent transatlantic cable. *Below*, the arrival of the cable at Heart's Content Bay, Newfoundland, on 27 July 1866.

Sir George Etienne Cartier.

Sir John A. Macdonald.

George Brown.

It has been said with some truth that the real Father of Canadian Federation was domestic deadlock, that the scheme of a federal union was the product of continued bitter racial and sectional conflict within Durham's United Canada. Admittedly, one of the main impulses was the deep-seated resolve on the part of both unhappy Canadian partners to break the contract that bound them together. And it is probable that a union of the Maritime provinces would have been the only result had not the wheels of administration in Canada come to a stand-still. But such an admission in no way alters the fact that the project of a Canadian nation must have proved abortive had not the British government in 1864 suddenly withdrawn its objections, and thrown its weight behind the proponents of a comprehensive federation. Fear of American designs, at a time when the North possessed the largest army in the world, was the decisive catalyst. It forced a reversal of British official policy, without which all the efforts and sacrifices of colonial statesmen like George Cartier, John A. Macdonald and George Brown would have been in vain.

American historians have shown that Northern politicians who cried out for annexation during and immediately after the Civil War, and who frightened British ministers into changing their minds were less interested in acquiring British colonial territory than in gaining political advantages at home. None the less, the rhetorical oratory of Manifest Destiny was as effective a spur to British action as if it had been administered with honest deliberation. British ministers met the challenge in the only way possible at the time. They decided to gamble. A patchwork of diverse settlements pulled together as a single state might, in their view, have a reasonable chance of survival; isolated provinces left to their separate resources would be tempting morsels which a hungry Republic could consume piecemeal as opportunity offered. A consolidated colony would, at least on paper, appear to offer a stronger front to would-be aggressors, and with luck the young federation might be granted time to grow strong and stand on its own feet. Perhaps unconsciously, British statesmen sensed that the creation of a nation in embryo might in the long run mean a partial shift of responsibility, and a consequent reduction of friction with the United States.

An anti-annexation cartoon of 1869.
Mrs Britannia: 'Is it possible, my dear, that
you have ever given your Cousin Jonathan
any encouragement?'
Miss Canada: 'Certainly not, Mamma, I
have told him we can never be united.'
(Cousin Jonathan later became Uncle Sam.)

Whatever the motives that governed British actions after the Civil War, the British North America Act which produced the Canadian federation of Ontario, Quebec, Nova Scotia and New Brunswick was a gigantic speculation. Migrations from the United Kingdom after the War of 1812 had helped to fill out the Maritime provinces, but increased prosperity in no way reduced a distinctive regional outlook that was almost national in its expression. Apart from lumber, fish and Cape Breton coal, the Atlantic provinces were not rich in economic resources, and the disparity in wealth and opportunity, as compared with Ontario and Quebec, accentuated the sensitivity that geography had originated. 'We are sold to Canada for the price of a sheep-skin': this was the dismal cry that followed a contrived union, which many regarded as a slick Canadian trick. As late as 1886, the premier of Nova Scotia won a general election on a platform which called for the repeal of the British North America Act.

British
North America
Act

133

Joseph Howe.

The Canadian West

In Quebec the racial fears of a minority, which George Cartier had done so much to stem, had not abated. Passionately intent on preserving their separate way of life, the French looked with suspicion on a central government that might tamper with their special privileges. Although the British North America Act had strengthened the guarantees provided by the Quebec Act, safeguarding local control of education, marriage, property and civil rights, the residuum of power lay with the federal authority. Thenceforward, the maintenance and the extension of provincial rights became for Quebec a matter of life and death in the struggle for cultural survival.

Most British Canadians were descendants of immigrants who had come to the country in the nineteenth century, and their attachment to the mother country deeply affected their conception of Canada's role within the British Empire. But French Canadians who had been North Americans for over three hundred years, and whose sentimental ties with France had been abandoned long ago, had no such divided allegiance. In a negative sense, they were supporters of the Empire because Westminster guaranteed their unique privileges as a minority within the Canadian nation. At the same time, they remained a prickly and highly self-conscious bloc, determined to resist any attempt to strengthen the connection with Great Britain.

Meanwhile, alarmed by the prospect of losing the West to acquisitive American settlers and fur traders, Canadian politicians, supported by British and local railway interests began to urge the immediate acquisition of the prairies and the extension of the railway system as far as the Pacific coast. Two hundred and fifty thousand square miles of Hudson's Bay Company territory were at stake, 'out of which,' declared Nova Scotia's tribune, Joseph Howe, 'five or six noble provinces may be formed. . . . I am neither a prophet, nor a son of a prophet, yet I believe that many in this room will live to hear the whistle of the steam-engine in the passes of the Rocky Mountains, and to make the journey from Halifax to the Pacific in five or six days.'

In 1860 the Grand Trunk Railway ran only from Sarnia on Lake Huron to Rivière du Loup on the St Lawrence River, 120 miles below Quebec. Three years later, an imaginative reorganization scheme, which

This procession of Ursulines in Quebec (*above*) shows the hold of European tradition as compared with the life of a Hudson's Bay Company trading settlement, such as Fort Garry, near Winnipeg (*below*).

Immigrants to the West at Dead Horse Creek, 53 miles west of Red River.

had the support of British bankers, contemplated its extension round Lake Superior, south of the Great Shield, to the old Red River colony on the outskirts of present-day Winnipeg; thence, in advance of rail-head, the route was to be traced by road and telegraph line to the settlements on the Pacific.

This attenuated project offered but meagre means of trans-continental communication; on the other hand, even the flimsiest physical ties might be important if the West were to be spared engulfment by encroaching swarms of American settlers. From Minnesota alone hundreds of immigrants were wearing a trail to the Red River colony which Lord Selkirk had planted for his Orkney Islanders between 1812 and 1813. Alarmed by the influx, the Hudson's Bay Company found increasing embarrassment in dealing with frontier elements, whose vigorous presence betokened increased American interest and influence.

Across the Rocky Mountains, the situation had been even more critical. Here, as on the prairies, rudimentary administration tottered as trading posts expanded into thriving settlements. A crisis developed quickly when the discovery of gold in the Fraser River started a wild rush of American and other foreign prospectors and gamblers. The immediate intervention of the British government and the creation of

Railway station at Victoria, B.C., 1876.

The main street of Barkerville, B.C., in the 1860s.

British Columbia in 1858 were the result. The next step was the transfer of the Hudson's Bay prairies to the Canadian government in 1869, and with this annexation of the North-West, the way was open for British Columbia to become, albeit with wary reluctance, a province in the Dominion of Canada.

British Columbia accepted the invitation because she was offered unexpectedly generous terms, most tempting of which was the federal government's promise to begin a connecting railway within two years and to finish it within ten. By 1876 the Intercolonial between Halifax and Quebec was complete, but political corruption combined with economic depression slowed building operations to a snail's pace. Not until 1880 did a reorganized Canadian Pacific Railway Company make a belated effort to fulfil the government's pledge. Under the direction of a brilliant American-born engineer, William Van Horne, the plateau of rock and scrub and swamp north of Lake Superior was conquered; then, at headlong speed, the line was pushed across the prairies south of the Saskatchewan Valley as far as Calgary, and finally, in 1883, up fearful gradients, more than five thousand feet above sea-level, through the Kicking Horse Pass; thence through the Selkirks and down the valley of the Fraser River to the Pacific Ocean.

Dawson, Yukon, in the 1890s during the gold rush.

On 7 November 1885 in Eagle Pass, Donald Smith (subsequently Lord Strathcona), one of that great company of Scots Canadian pioneers and builders, drove home the last spike. 'Oatmeal was in their blood,' wrote the Canadian poet E. J. Pratt:

Their names were like a battle-muster – Angus
(He of the Shops) and Fleming (of the Transit),
Hector (of the Kicking Horse), Dawson,
'Cromart' Ross and Beatty (Ulster Scot),
Bruce, Allan, Galt and Douglas, and the 'twa' –
Stephen (Craigellachie) and Smith (Strathcona)

Towards the Last Spike, Toronto, 1952

At long last Champlain's North-West Passage was a reality; an efficient route to the Far East had been established, and even more significant, a clutter of regional segments was now bound together, however tenuously, into a coast-to-coast national entity.

'The Last Spike'. The railway from Vancouver to Montreal was symbolically completed by Donald Smith at Craigellachie in Eagle Pass, B.C., 1885.

The Canadian Pacific Railway in 1886 advertising its role as the Empire's link between the Atlantic and the Pacific.

138

ENGLAND'S KEY TO HER ASIATIC & AUSTRALASIAN POSSESSIONS

IS CANADA, AND MUST USE THE
CANADIAN PACIFIC RAILWAY,
(The only line from the Atlantic to the Pacific)
TO REACH THEM
ON TIME.

The first through passenger train from the Atlantic to the Pacific at Port Arthur, 30 June 1886 (*top*); and a cheap-rate 'colonist car' used to transport immigrants to the West (*above*).

Kicking Horse Pass, B.C., during construction of the railway, 1884.

THE OLD FLAG.
THE OLD POLICY.
THE OLD LEADER.

John A. Macdonald,
first Prime Minister of Federal Canada,
died shortly after winning the election of 1891
for which this poster was published.

Yet American acceptance of the fact that the North American continent might conceivably be shared between republic and monarchy was an attitude of slow growth. 'I know,' Secretary of State W. H. Seward remarked at the end of the Civil War, 'that Nature designs that this whole continent . . . shall be, sooner or later, within the magic circle of the American Union.' It was expected that tariff pressures alone would gradually build up annexation sentiment. Against such aggressive tactics, Canadians had few resources to throw into the scales, apart from the weight and bargaining power of Great Britain. Moreover, the long list of boundary concessions and surrenders that marked the course of British diplomacy from 1783 to 1871 gave them scant confidence in their champion.

John A. Macdonald   The first Prime Minister of Canada, John A. Macdonald, was sufficient of a statesman and opportunist to realize that British ministers were in no position to push Canadian interests to the limit of war. In terms of Natural Law, Macdonald was right when he exclaimed in a moment of pique that his country had been sacrificed in almost every Anglo-American treaty concerned with British North America. Yet he knew that Canada had much more to lose from a just war than from an unjust treaty. Outraged Canadians might curse the timidity of British appeasers, as they did in 1903 when the terms of the notorious Alaska Boundary award were made public, but Macdonald knew that Canadians, if left to their own resources, had no means of safeguarding the national existence at all.

There was one short-lived war scare in 1895 following President Cleveland's 'Venezuela challenge', but it blew over quickly, and serious international questions that once smelled of dynamite disappeared with it. The border that had quaked under crises for one hundred years achieved its present peaceful demeanour before the nineteenth century had run its course.

None the less, the United States remained arrogantly protectionist, and the continued failure of Canadian governments to break American tariff barriers at a time when the home manufacturer was suffering from increased American competition, forced the Macdonald government to consider some form of protection as a measure of civil defence. Obviously a substantial tariff system would not open doors to new markets, but the new 'National Policy', as it was called, did appeal to patriotic Canadians whose repeated pilgrimages to Washington had met with constant rebuff. Whether the National Policy tariff of 1878 brought the country real benefit, apart from an enhanced sense of nationality, may be doubted. There was little time for the experiment to prove itself. During the long depression of the 1880s commercial union with the United States was openly discussed, and to faint-hearted observers, the creation of a common continental economy seemed inevitable. While the United States grew by leaps and bounds, Canada moved lethargically, or stood still.

Between 1871 and 1901 a Canadian population of some three and a half millions increased at a rate of probably less than sixty thousand a year. European immigrants were running out almost as rapidly as they had entered. By 1901 more than a million and a half residents of Canada had departed across the border to find a higher standard of living.

A farm on the Western frontier.

A cartoonist of 1870 speculates on the future of the Red River Settlement, which was shortly to become Manitoba.

New immigrants from Galicia on a farm at Stuarton, Manitoba.

Prime Minister Wilfrid Laurier in Edmonton leading the cheering on 1 September 1905 at the inauguration ceremony of the province of Alberta.

But with the opening of the new century, suddenly as by a miracle all was changed. Economic conditions improved rapidly, and likewise self-confidence in a Canadian future. 'The Twentieth Century belongs to Canada': so said Wilfrid Laurier when under his banner the Liberals swept to power in 1896. Twenty-five years earlier, apart from Indians, scarcely more than twelve thousand people lived in the western territories (hitherto owned by the Hudson's Bay Company), and most of these were fur traders. By 1901, with the opening of virgin lands and free homesteads, the population had grown to more than four hundred thousand. During the next decade settlers from eastern Canada, the United States and Europe swarmed into the prairies at the rate of two and three hundred thousand a year, permitting the creation of two new provinces, Alberta and Saskatchewan, in 1905 (Manitoba had been so organized in 1870). By 1911, despite the lethal assaults of hail, grasshoppers, drought and rust, the wide, flat ribbon stretching from Winnipeg to the foothills of the Rocky Mountains contained more than 1,300,000 souls.

Populating the Prairies

143

Temporary headquarters of a
real estate office in Vancouver, 1885;
the coming of the railway
created a boom.

First train of the Grand Trunk Pacific Railway into Strathcona Depot and Edmonton.

British capital and American techniques were plentifully supplied to accelerate the task of sowing and reaping the wheatlands. New industries were added, and by a tragic error for which national optimism and party politics must be held responsible, two new railway systems were projected: the National Transcontinental (to be linked by lease with a subsidiary of the Grand Trunk, the Grand Trunk Pacific), providing a through-line from Moncton, New Brunswick, to Prince Rupert on the Pacific coast; and a private western network, the Canadian Northern, which by 1915 had bought up sufficient links in central Canada to complete a transcontinental railway from Quebec to Vancouver. The enormous costs of delirious expansion, chiefly borne by the Canadian government, were not justified by the achievement; both systems were to be subsequently salvaged at the expense of the tax-payer, and merged under the name of the Canadian National Railways.

Laying tracks on the Shield.

New settlers in Alberta, 1906.

It was a period of unparalleled prosperity, and the Laurier railway policy, as W. L. Morton has deftly expressed it, was simply 'the supreme expression of Canadian national importance'. Dominion affairs had ceased to be 'pump politics'; the era of prize-day speeches on the future greatness of Canada had begun. Just as the expansion of the American frontier helped to foster an American confidence and cockiness, so did the peopling of the Canadian prairies give stimulus to Canadian imperial impulses. Eastern Canada, the northern United States and the British Isles supplied the vanguard, but the government was soon persuaded to tap the immense labour reservoirs of central and south-east Europe, and under the aegis of the Minister of the Interior, Clifford Sifton, Ruthenians, Poles, Doukhobors and Ukranians were

Immigrants landing at the port of Quebec were transferred directly into trains for the West.

hurried westward by ship and train. The Ukranians of Austria-Hungary and Russia were the largest group, and as co-operative farmers, probably the most successful. They brought with them not only stout hearts and skilled hands, but a rich heritage of folk-music, handicrafts, and traditional customs, which the North American melting-pot has fortunately not yet dissolved.

Meanwhile, at the end of the most auspicious decade in Canadian history, the Canadian Prime Minister had finally negotiated what every government had sought since Confederation: a reciprocity trade pact with the United States in the natural produce of farm, forest, river and mine. President Taft was anxious to give the Canadians a good bargain in the hope of extinguishing the last embers of ill-will that boundary

Wilfrid Laurier.

Nationalism

disputes and United Empire Loyalist resentments had kept alive. He was eager to establish his country as 'the Good Neighbour'. Unhappily, the agreement encountered much opposition in Congress, and it was only forced through by maladroit use of the argument that a reciprocity treaty was a practical step towards continental union. Such rhetoric was intended for home consumption, but the main impact was felt in Canada. Even without the confusion precipitated in Quebec by Laurier's decision to build a Canadian navy, the threat of Manifest Destiny was sufficient to ensure the defeat of the Liberal government in the general election of 1911. Impelled by a new sense of national kinship, the Canadian people rose in revolt against an arrangement that suggested peaceful annexation. Even the little man was prepared to pay more for his bacon or his bicycle rather than have his country's independence jeopardized.

Not unnaturally, Americans were amazed and perplexed by this unexpected and vigorous outburst of national feeling. It was obviously difficult for them to take Canadian nationhood seriously. Most of the formal official contacts were made through the British Embassy in Washington, and this view of a colonial satellite was confirmed by the ostentatious presence of red pillar-boxes, Guards' uniforms, Union Jacks, and the fervent response of Toronto audiences to renderings of the British national anthem. Yet the spawn of European imperialism proved to have an individuality of its own and an almost jingoistic national spirit – anti-American no doubt, but only in the sense that Canadians were determined to preserve a free hand in working out their own destiny. Amid the conflicts of power and diplomacy which had repeatedly tested Anglo-American relations since the War of 1812, a scattered collection of provinces and territories had managed to survive American absorption on the one hand, and any demeaning form of imperial servitude on the other. In the process, a mixed colonial society had achieved, without armed revolution, a separate political identity on the North American continent.

148

Chapter Seven

Twice before 1914 Canadians were to draw their swords, but barely half-way from the scabbard: once in 1869 when a token French Canadian force went to Rome to help Pope Pius IX defend his enclave against the nationalists, and again in 1899 when an English-speaking contingent set out for South Africa. But these were far-away adventures which barely touched domestic life. Canadians lived a sheltered existence in an apparently fire-proof house, and under the canopy of British power had achieved a unique position of independence within an Empire. Energized by their conquest of the western prairies and braced by faith in continued peaceful progress, they were totally unprepared when the thunderbolt of world war fell, much as it did in Britain, from cloudless skies. By December 1914, exactly a hundred years after the settlement of Ghent, some thirty-two thousand Canadian troops, including artillery services, were under canvas on Salisbury Plain. The arrival of the first expeditionary force was the starting-point for the most momentous adventure in Canadian history.

First World War

Canada went to war when Britain went to war; the decision was constitutionally automatic. Yet the unofficial reaction, except in the province of Quebec, was instantaneous and vigorous. Although a growing national self-consciousness had begun to confuse the traditional impulses of colonial loyalty, no substantial element in the population

149

The Royal Canadian Regiment and the 1st Gordon Highlanders fording the Modder River in February 1900 during the Boer War.

Canadian soldiers on Salisbury Plain during the First World War about to be reviewed by George V.

wanted to cut the imperial tie. Even Quebec, which remained fearful of English-speaking ascendancy, preferred Westminster to Ottawa as the lesser evil. In Ontario, school textbooks still carried pictures of Their Britannic Majesties on the frontispiece, or coloured Union Jacks with the motto: One Flag, One Fleet, One Throne. The year 1914 marked no specific break with the past. A British dominion went to war, content to leave unanswered, for the time being, ambiguous questions of legal status.

In the long run, active participation in the European war was to hasten world recognition of Canada as a nation, and to confirm her independence even in the field of foreign affairs. But in 1916 the home

front seemed far more important in the eyes of many Ottawa politicians than the shell-shattered lines that ran from Arras to the Belgian coast. The decision of the Prime Minister, Sir Robert Borden, to adopt selective conscription as a means of meeting the urgent need for reinforcements overseas suddenly revealed the dangerous stresses imposed by racial division on the fragile structure of Canadian society. In French Canada, the introduction of the Military Service Act was damned as a betrayal, and Ontario 'Prussianism' suddenly took on greater meaning for political orators than German militarism. The province of Quebec, cried Henri Bourassa, leader of the Nationalists, had become 'the Verdun of French civilization in America'.

The 101st Battalion leaving Edmonton, Alberta, for Europe in 1914.

The town of Namur after the entry of Canadian cavalry in November 1918.

Canadian soldiers marching their German prisoners through a French town after the Battle of Vimy Ridge, April 1917.

Sir Robert Borden, Prime Minister of Canada, with Brigadier-General Macdonnell, Commander of the 1st Canadian Division, taking the salute in France, March 1917.

But these strains within the body politic had been chronic since Confederation. Any dramatic incident was sufficient to explode the latent passions of an ever-watchful minority. When Louis Riel was executed in 1885 for leading an insurrection of western Indians and French Canadian half-breeds who feared white civilization and the loss of their ancestral lands, a violent agitation swept the province. To the French Canadian, Riel's death was a vicious blow delivered by English Canada against the Confederation ideal of equal partnership. Fifteen years later when the Boer War broke out, Quebec's resistance to military engagements overseas was token evidence of French Canadian determination to avoid involvement in *L'Imperialisme* and English-Canadian wars. When 1917 arrived, the government's necessary but inept efforts at compulsion froze a suspicious and fearful people into solid opposition, and left a legacy of resentments that festered below the surface until the crisis of a second world war opened the old wound.

As a result of the disturbances produced by the Conscription issue, the Canadian contribution in manpower scarcely compared favourably with that of other Dominions. On the other hand, out of her small population of nine million, six hundred thousand (chiefly of British birth and origin) joined the expeditionary forces, and of these, some sixty thousand were left dead in France and Flanders. For the first time, the country had accepted heavy military responsibilities and corres

CANADA!
YPRES: APRIL 22–24, 1915.

The Canadian soldier
at the Battle of Ypres
from *Punch*, 5 May 1915.

154

ponding sacrifices, and this assertion of maturity directly enhanced her international status.

Once the war was over, Sir Robert Borden was able, with the support of other Dominion leaders, to insist on membership in the Peace Conference, and only when the treaties had been passed by Parliament did the Canadian government ratify them. This victory was confirmed by admission to a seat in the new League of Nations, along with the right of membership in the Council. Although as isolationist as the United States in fundamental purpose, Canada regarded membership in the League as the first step towards world recognition, and thanks to a liberal interpretation of Article X of the Covenant, she was able to assert herself with little risk of being asked to fulfil any military obligation overseas.

Sir Robert Borden.

Thenceforward, there was no holding a country intent on burying its colonial past. Imperial Federation belonged in the lumber-room of lost causes. During the 1920s, Canada was able to insist that her own commercial policy and her own foreign policy should be formulated and implemented separately from those of the United Kingdom. In any future war, declared the Prime Minister in 1922, Parliament would decide whether circumstances dictated Canadian participation. But would neutrality be compatible with the imperial connection which Canadians were still anxious to preserve? In other words, could an empire exist without a common foreign policy? Obviously a centralized imperial federation such as Joseph Chamberlain had dreamed about was not only dead but damned. A new formula of union had to be invented which would satisfy the aspirations of sensitive nationalists without disrupting a cherished British association.

The discovery of this formula during the Imperial Conference of 1926 initiated a new era of Commonwealth relations. It has been said that Lord Balfour in the course of a meeting suddenly scratched the magic words on the back of an old envelope: The Dominions and Great Britain 'are autonomous Communities within the British Empire, equal in status, in no way subordinate one to another in any aspect of their domestic or external affairs, though united by a common allegiance to the Crown and freely associated as members of the British

Empire to Commonwealth

155

At the 1926 Imperial Conference which defined the status of the Dominions, in the front row from left to right: Stanley Baldwin, George V, and William Lyon Mackenzie King.

Commonwealth of Nations'. The Conference endorsed without qualification this happily ambiguous declaration of national equality. Five years later it was given legal confirmation by the Statute of Westminster. Imperial control over Dominions' affairs had been reduced to the level of a pedant's quibble. Canada had reached the Promised Land of independence.

But beyond this pronouncement of egalitarian principle and practice, not much happened. Nicholas Murray Butler, President of Columbia University, hailed the Statute as the greatest constitutional achievement since the Declaration of American Independence; but equality in law was not the same thing as equality of function. At her own wish, Canada was given no direct control over the amendment of her own constitution, and owing to provincial fears of federal trespass, she still lacks the necessary constituent authority. In 1947 the Judicial Committee of the Privy Council had to insist, against the objections of

In 1949 the Canadian Supreme Court in Ottawa became the final court of interpretation and appeal.

Ontario, Quebec, New Brunswick and British Columbia, on the competence of the Canadian Parliament to abolish appeals to London. Not until two years later did the Supreme Court of Canada assume the right of passing final judgment on all cases involving the interpretation of Canadian laws.

As for external affairs, the personnel of the Department which Laurier had founded in 1909 was increased only slightly. Although the office of High Commissioner had been established in London as early as 1880, not until after the First World War were the first three Canadian legations opened at Washington, Paris and Tokyo. Elsewhere, Canada remained dependent upon the experienced diplomatic and consular services of the United Kingdom. For this reason, certain colonial habits of mind persisted. Preoccupation with matters of status was not of itself sufficient to make the long-sought image of confident nationhood a reality.

On the other hand, concentration on status probably accounted for the temporary reaction from British influence which expressed itself during the 1930s in captious attacks on British imperialism. A British Commonwealth bloc, said the Prime Minister William Lyon Mackenzie King, who was determined to avoid all commitments and military sanctions, would excite resentful opposition throughout the world. His lead was followed by numerous converts to the new nationalism who felt obliged to couple the story of Canada's liberation from the imperial yoke with expositions of the country's predominantly North American culture, and the need for close relations with the United States. 'The cardinal thesis of that (nationalist) school', wrote the scholarly editor of *The Montreal Star*, 'was that at all costs Canada had to fight its way out from under the traditional influence of British imperialist and colonial rule: and that one of the best ways of doing it was to use the influence of the United States.'

It took another world war to dissipate this academic *malaise* and reveal that pro-British sentiment was still a potent factor in influencing Canadian external policy. Yet British sentiment could not be the all-compelling factor it had been in 1914 when half the country's fighting men were British-born. By 1939 the population was a little more than twelve million, of which only half stemmed from Anglo-Saxon stock. Slightly less than thirty per cent were French-speaking; about twenty per cent were of recent European origin – Ukranians, Poles, Germans and Scandinavians. Immigration from the United Kingdom had fallen to a trickle, and the character of the country was far less British than North American. Consequently, the Canadian government's declaration of war, one week after Britain, was an indirect but deliberate declaration of national independence. Despite the murmurings of isolationists who favoured 'passive belligerency', and the efforts of the Prime Minister of Quebec to exploit the traditional anti-imperial sentiment of his province, a North American nation, not a British dominion, rejected neutrality and went to war of its own volition on 10 September.

The salient feature of the period between the wars had been the remarkable growth of national autonomy. But despite her advanced status, Canada appears to have had less influence on high policy matters

Normandy landing of Canadian troops, June 1944.

Canadian tanks driving through the streets of an Italian city.

Navy memorial to the dead of two world wars above Halifax Harbour.

between 1939 and 1945 than during the First World War. Her role as interpreter between the two great kindred powers was a very minor one; neither Britain nor the United States called her to their councils. There was a partnership in name, but in practice the main direction of military affairs within North America was provided by the United States. This unilateral surrender of part of her sovereignty was in considerable degree the result of unpreparedness, for which the Prime Minister Mackenzie

King must be held largely responsible. Protected by a powerful neigh-bour and insulated from Europe by a wide ocean, Canadians were less concerned about security than other nations, and under the spell of the League of Nations wherein membership brought prestige and status with a minimum of obligation and effort, the government was reluctant to undertake long-range military programmes, or, even in the year before the outbreak, provide airfield training facilities for the R.A.F. As a result, when the United States entered the war in 1941, not only was Canada's importance as a British ally reduced, she was almost wholly dependent upon her neighbour for protection against external aggression.

Historians have credited King with a capacity for ruthless political *Mackenzie King* action and a considerable astuteness in protecting Canadian interests and autonomy. A prime minister of Canada has also to be a conciliator, and Laurier had drilled home the lesson that the vital object in all circumstances was the preservation of Canadian unity, which meant in broad essentials a constant understanding and skilful cultivation of the French Canadian point of view. By sticking to Laurier during the Conscription crisis of 1917, Mackenzie King had inherited Quebec. No longer suspected of anti-clericalism by the Catholic hierarchy, less enamoured of the trappings of Empire and Commonwealth and less tempted by ingratiating pedlars of imperial unity, the Liberals con-tinued to hold Quebec much as the American Democrats acquired a monopoly of the 'Solid South'. Since 1897 the Liberal Party was accepted as the more dependable guardian of provincial prerogatives and cultural interests, and until 1957 it was able to win a majority of Quebec votes in every election. The Quebec alliance made King the leader of what became in reality a ruling dynasty.

Lacking both the personal magnetism of Laurier and the winning roguishness of Macdonald, this podgy and uninspiring intellectual whose speeches were usually peppered with moral platitudes, managed to win elections with a constancy that gave him a reputation for political infallibility. Morbidly cautious by nature, he shunned all divisive issues and promulgated no significant political principles except that of national unity, with which under divine guidance he identified his own destiny and that of his administration.

Second World War　　There was a moment of agony in 1944, when the Conscription issue broke out again, owing to a false appreciation of the German *blitzkrieg* and underestimation of infantry wastage figures. Yet King was able to push through a mild measure of compulsory service. As no one else, he managed to hold together the fragile *entente* with Quebec, aided by the errors of his opponents, his traditional good luck and the timely ending of the European war. The full manpower story with its political implications has yet to be told. Whatever the final judgment may be, the King doctrine of 'national unity at all costs' weathered the storm to become enshrined as a patriotic cliché. But in the far future, historians may find it symbolic of an era when astute politicians paid lip-service to valour, and called practical expediency national idealism.

> *Truly he will be remembered,*
> *(wrote Montreal's F.R. Scott)*
> *Wherever men honour ingenuity,*
> *Ambiguity, inactivity and political longevity.*
>
> F.R. Scott and A.J.M. Smith, *The Blasted Pine*
> (An anthology of Canadian satiric verse), Toronto, 1957

Canada's contribution to the war was materially substantial and effectual. Considering the country's uneven geographic structure and divided population it represented a major achievement. But it was not on a scale that entitled the nation to rank, as Mackenzie King once put it, in 'perfect equality of status', with the major powers. None the less, when peace came, largely in consequence of the revolution in her industrial life, the so-called 'arsenal of democracy' stood in fourth place as a trading and industrial nation. Despite limitations imposed by a comparatively small population – less than fourteen million in 1949 – she was able, because of the resources at her disposal, to exercise a considerable international influence in the years following 1945.

International Prestige　　Unhappily, the special circumstances which accounted for her unique post-war activity were not to endure. The recovery of devastated Europe and Asia – especially Japan – in the early 1950s, by ending Canadian post-war prosperity reduced her relative prestige in the councils of the world. Although the approach continued to be vigorous, and the pursuit of status by exhortation and example still fervent, inevitably the views of Canadians in the New York forum of the United Nations became less seriously regarded. Tidy compromise is not the key to the solution of every international problem. Yet for reasons of national expediency Canada preferred the international stage to the British Commonwealth club-room. Liberal governments were prepared to accept the new Commonwealth as 'a worthy association of well-wishers', whose prime ministers met regularly and decorously as at mothers' meetings, but Mackenzie King and his immediate successors found it politically safer to propound a foreign policy in terms of universal security rather than through an association that still smelled, in the nostrils of French Canada, acridly of empire.

It was important that Canadian policy should have the widest, and at the same time the least divisive appeal to a heterogenous nation, of which the Anglo-Saxon proportion was less than fifty per cent. Because of racial divergencies it was wiser to support policies of universal security through the United Nations or NATO than to play a positive role as senior Dominion at the Commonwealth conference table.

When the storm over Suez rocked the Commonwealth in 1956, official emphasis remained, as before, on peace, not the enforcement of peace. The popular acclaim which greeted Mr Lester Pearson's eager intervention as 'honest broker' was much welcomed in Ottawa, but it was not accompanied by any lasting increase of international influence. Moral strictures and · military contrivances on the part of Canada's Minister for External Affairs could not alter the fact that the use of force, even through the United Nations, was not a basic Canadian interest. Without the will or the power to back up moral judgments, any serious approach to leadership in international affairs was a delusion. A small country, which was reluctant, in the interest of national unity, to pay for some form of military service could scarcely count on strengthening its position in the councils of the world.

Within Canada, popular attachment to principles of international co-operation is widespread and sincere; yet there is no need to over-idealize the foreign policy of recent Canadian governments. Shorn of moral pretentiousness their attitude is based on two major considerations:

one, the racial cleavage for which the international arena provides an escape, and second, the country's subordinate relationship to a benevolent but dominating neighbour, a relationship which could, at the worst, lead to complete dependence on the strength and wishes of another society.

The old principle of national preservation based on a balance between two powers of almost equal resources was a thing of the past. British power had diminished, that of the United States had enormously increased. In the eyes of most Canadians the chief danger of the future lay not, as during the nineteenth century, in the threat of American imperialism, but in the growing weight of American cultural and economic influence.

In terms of actual space Canada is larger than her neighbour, but the United States has ten times Canada's population and more than a dozen times her wealth in terms of national income. As a result of the tremendous inflow of capital, American investments in Canada form the largest single bloc outside American borders (the United States is almost completely dependent on Canada for nickel, asbestos and newsprint). It has been estimated that more than sixty-five per cent of the Canadian economy is owned by citizens of the United States. Industries such as the motor-car, electrical apparatus, petroleum, rubber, pulp and paper, are almost entirely American-owned, and in greater measure controlled by appointed boards of directors or managers. Even the destinies of the Canadian trade unionist may be affected by negotiations and settlements that concern his own or his employer's affairs only remotely. The political implications have naturally enough been felt in every province and particularly at Ottawa. The late President Kennedy's interest in Canadian elections was indirect but obvious.

Before the Second World War, the United Kingdom had supplied about twenty per cent of Canada's imports: in 1955 the figure was eight, and more recently about five per cent. In 1964 Canada bought from Britain less than half as much as Britain bought from Canada. On the other hand, partly as a consequence of falling British competition, about sixty-six per cent of Canadian trade flowed to the United States. The prospect of becoming more closely tied to her neighbour has naturally

The building of this hydro-electric generating station, which spans the St Lawrence with plants on each shore, was a joint Canadian-United States enterprise.

been disturbing to Canadians, who can look forward to heavy trading deficits once the balancing inflow of American investment capital ceases.

In these circumstances, it has been frequently urged that Britain should restore the balance by adopting more efficient export methods and a more enterprising sales' technique. But such an argument ignores the immense difficulty of reaching, from across the seas, twenty million people along some four thousand miles of American border between

Newfoundland and Vancouver Island, people who have been over the years educated to American consumer standards ranging from cars to hot dogs. The twenty-one-gun salute that greeted the opening of the St Lawrence Seaway to ocean shipping in 1959, did little to relieve the despondency of British manufacturers who had for so long been lectured on their failure to penetrate the Canadian market.

It is impossible to exaggerate the advantages of propinquity – the subtle and overpowering pressures exercised by American radio networks, television, press releases and magazines through the medium of a language that most people can understand. Canadians read the same kind of newspapers, spend the same kind of money, watch the same television programmes, use the same slang (and profanity), laugh at the same comic strips, worship the same baseball stars and play the same games.

Moreover, as a direct consequence of scientific advances, the two countries have been forced into a military partnership, which can, under American direction, have no fixed limit. The requirements of North American defence resulting from the discovery of the atom and hydrogen bombs and the perfection of long-range airborne missiles have inevitably meant a certain sacrifice of Canadian sovereignty. The United States for the sake of its own security is determined that the North-West Territories shall not give ready access to the invader who plots a course over the Arctic. Consequently, Washington has taken the line, benevolently but firmly, that joint precautions in terms of highways, troops and radar networks must be taken to render the northern defences as tight as science and human ingenuity can make them. The Permanent Joint Defence Board of 1940 was the first official recognition of an arrangement that was elaborated after the war to promote the standardization of equipment, training and tactics, and to provide for the 'mutual availability' of military bases. The co-ordination of air forces was achieved in 1957, when NORAD – the North American Air Defence Command – was organized to permit instant engagement in the event of attack.

With eyes still turned inwards to the Valley of the St Lawrence, the French Canadian was unlikely, however, to show much enthusiasm for bilateral defence arrangements. An overpowering but nervous ally might, in an emergency, demand a more equal sharing of burdens, and suggest some form of conscription for military service; the United States might request, as in fact she did, that the nuclear deterrent should be jointly available as part of the northern defences.

Yet the tendency of French Canada to submit to alien incursions had been growing since the First World War. The once cloistered land of Maria Chapdelaine was succumbing reluctantly but gradually to the engines and instruments of North American 'big business'. After 1774 Quebec had determinedly girded herself as a fortress in defence of French Canadian cultural identity. For almost a century and a half the walls had held firm. By the 1920s, however, it was apparent that industry and finance had moved subtly and insidiously through the crumbling walls of the beleaguered province. One by one the ramparts had been breached by the assault troops of *les intérêts de la finance anglaise*. And the traditional character of a peasant society was bending under the weight of large-scale monopolistic industries – aluminium, newsprint, mining, chemical and aircraft – in which French Canadians played only a minor part as compared with English-speaking owners and directors.

Lack of business acumen and initiative was partly responsible for this subordinate role in commerce and industry, and it would be a mistake to assume that the French Canadians were the victims of conscious racial discrimination. Indeed, from the days of Baldwin to Mackenzie King, Canadian prime ministers have been repeatedly subject to French Canadian persuasion, simply because the Quebec vote was essential if they were to stay in power. None the less, two conscription crises and the continued domination of English and American commercial interests have made the Quebecois increasingly sensitive about their minority status. Inevitably the old cry 'Quebec for the French Canadians' rose again – and with increasing anguish in the middle 1960s – as embittered leaders talked intermittently about secession. Such a fashionable solution, in view of the province's geographical and economic position, is unlikely; nevertheless, the challenge of resurgent Quebec, coming in a period of weak and inept national leadership, imposes heavy strains on the Canadian body politic.

The post-war invasion by European and other immigrants, which brought the population from under thirteen to nearly twenty millions in twenty years, further complicated administration in the domestic field. The process of producing from the melting-pot something like a one hundred per cent North American was naturally accelerated in every region except Quebec. Consequently, the average Canadian of 1967 bears little resemblance to his predecessor who fought for King and Country in 1914, or even the emerging nationalist of 1939.

His culture, unlike that of the United States, is still influenced by a British heritage, especially apparent in the character of the constitution, the administration of justice, political party machinery and parliamentary practice. But the Canadian of the present generation depends for sustenance neither on British warships, British bankers, British markets nor British teachers. He enjoys a high standard of living comparable to that of the United States. He likes Americans individually, but fears them in the mass as enemies of Canadian sovereignty and Canadian culture. At the same time he is happy to accept the protective benefits of the Monroe Doctrine and a northern radar shield largely at American expense. Such guarantees of security help him to maintain the peaceful life, and to confirm a reputation for virtue which 'three thousand miles of unguarded frontier' had originally established.

Epilogue

One hundred years ago, the Fathers of Confederation faced the hazardous task of welding half a continent into a single state. They sought to create a nation, nourished on the traditions of parliamentary government, loyal to the Crown and independent of and clearly distinguishable from its thrusting neighbour, the United States. Today the foundations they laid seem to be shifting on slippery sands as Canada finds herself pressed inexorably into a smothering North American industrial complex, where cultures, ideas, attitudes and even racial peculiarities tend to become homogenized. In the words of a senior Canadian civil servant: 'We've had access to American know-how, British political wisdom, and French culture. Somehow we've managed to end up with British know-how, French political wisdom and American culture.'

It was fear of engulfment by monolithic American culture that was *Search* principally responsible for the appointment in 1949 of a Royal Com- *for Cultural* mission on National Development in the Arts, Letters and Sciences, *Identity* with Mr Vincent Massey as chairman. While granting the benefits of benevolent neighbourliness in terms of philanthropy and general intellectual stimulus, the authors of the final report were concerned about the lack of a unique Canadianism in arts and letters – a Canadian 'accent' equivalent to the Australian revelation of landscape, language and contemporary society. The failure of determined attempts to evolve distinct cultural interests could be largely explained, it was confessed, by the corrosive effects of radio, television, and magazine journalism from across the border, by the langüage and cultural differences – the emphasis on original ethnic traditions – which produced not only political disharmony but social uncertainty, and by a smug acceptance of the values inherent in a society rich in material things. 'The frontier view of the arts still prevails,' wrote Professor Roy Daniells in *The Culture of Contemporary Canada* (1957); 'they are regarded as light recreation, a brief diversion, a stimulus comparable to half a bottle of whiskey. . . .' Let us pray, cried that stormy petrel of Canadian *academia*, Professor Frank Underhill, that the post-war invasion of immigrants 'may liberate Toronto from its Anglican stuffiness and its Methodist piety, and that they may eventually bring to Ottawa something more creative than the distillation of our "moderation".'

Out of a background essentially colonial in character, the expression of a distinctly Canadian individuality or identity was a slow creation. The headlong rush towards prosperity, which started with the twentieth century, left little time for the exercise of creative talent, and the few souls who did eke a precarious livelihood from the arts naturally leaned on the methods and thoughts of the old masters. Sensitive perceptions and exuberant love of country were not sufficient of themselves to provide a maturity and originality that could only stem from deep learning and long experiment. None the less, the skills and techniques of an older tradition have been, within the last century, successfully adapted to the Canadian scene and transfused with the Canadian ethos. It was the 'Group of Seven', mainly young men, whose paintings first revealed the stark and desolate beauty of the Great Shield. Poets too, while by no means confining themselves to nature, obtained lyric inspiration in the majesty and haunting loneliness of northern lakes and forests.

But a 'Canadian accent' was almost bound to be a regional accent, whether of New Brunswick, the Yukon, the Glengarry country, or the western plains and mountains. French Canadian novelists provided no exception. Moved by their isolation in a corner of the Anglo-American continent, they spurned the patterns of their blood-brothers in France to

Outstanding among Canadian painters are the 'Group of Seven' who found their inspiration in the wilds of northern Ontario. Among them are J. E. H. MacDonald who painted *Autumn in Algoma* in 1921 (*right above*) and F. H. Varley *Some Day the People Will Return* in 1918 (*right*).

Examples of independent Canadian-born artists' work are *Purple Track* by Jean Paul Riopelle (*bottom left*) and *Tyranny of the Corner* (*Traffic Set*) by Harold Town (*bottom right*).

The Canada Council was established in 1957 to encourage all aspects of cultural and scholarly activity. It supports the Shakespeare Festival at Stratford, Ontario, whose theatre was opened in 1957.

strike out on their own, acquiring in the process a modest international audience, comparable to that of their English-speaking compatriots.

All told, however, developments in arts and letters did not provide the quality of cultural fare that Canadians could wish, and the Massey Commission faced with the threat of 'intellectual and moral annexation' from the United States had no hesitation in recommending substantial annual expenditure from the public revenue in defence of national culture. The Canadian Broadcasting Corporation, the National Film Board and federal institutions such as art galleries, libraries and museums benefited from the Commissioners' recommendations; but the most vitalizing proposal concerned 'the encouragement of the Arts, Letters, Humanities and Social Sciences'. The object of the Canada Council, which was established by government in 1957, was to improve conditions for productive scholarship in fields ranging from historical research to Eskimo sculpture and the ballet. Poets, philologists, painters, anthropologists and architects of distinction cannot be created by official benefactions, but such transfusions have given stimulus and hope to the deserving, and lent strength to the professional few. They have also helped to sustain one of Canada's most adventurous experiments in drama: the annual Shakespearian Festival in Stratford, Ontario.

Part of Canada's cultural heritage is preserved in the grounds of the University of British ▶ Columbia. Indian totem poles.

174   Place Ville Marie is a spectacular new town centre development in Montreal.

The record in the arts and social sciences is a creditable one, and the onlooker might well be puzzled that Canadians, after half a century of economic and political fulfilment, should worry so mightily about themselves: why has there been so much introspection and self-absorption? After two world wars Canadians had achieved immense prosperity and a dignified international status; yet they had not made their intended mark upon the world. They had successfully resisted all forms of physical integration with the United States; yet their destiny still seemed threatened by the oppressive weight of American hegemony.

It may be that the dual nature of Canadian administration, involving province and race, has inhibited the country from responding

Widespread interest turned to Montreal in 1967, to Canada's World Exhibition – Expo 67. One of the most exciting displays was this revolutionary housing complex designed by a young Canadian architect which remains a permanent feature of the city.

whole-heartedly and massively to an external situation which most people regret and resent. There is the more obvious and significant fact that the way to an expanding economy and great riches has been the path of least resistance. Any Canadian government would find it impossible to accept curbs on economic development in the interest of cultural nationhood. The life of Canada is too closely interwoven with that of the United States to permit anything approaching a positive independence. In trade, transportation and investment the two countries are irretrievably bound together.

Yet Canadian governments have collaborated on the whole amicably and effectively with their American counterparts. In peacetime, they have been able, thanks to vast natural resources, to play the client rather than the sycophant, not hesitating on occasion to remind Washington that the small neighbour should not be taken for granted as a poor relation. Indeed, the booming post-war economy proved to be an unrivalled diplomatic asset on the international stage. During the lustrous 1950s, the last remnants of the old colonial inferiority complex seemed to have been dropped behind the United Nations' footlights in New York. Canadians began to talk of their new maturity with a confidence suggesting that the twentieth century might still be theirs.

During the balmy Indian summer, literary critics wrote about the 'dynamic and fruitful tension between the dual cultural and religious traditions' – the happy willingness to accept and live within an uneasy balance of ever-changing domestic fortunes. But the effort to find strength through tension could not be sustained, and the eager pursuit of international recognition was insufficient to make the long-sought image of national greatness more than an illusion. The curse of domestic division remained. The political and emotional foundations of Quebec separatism have not been broken, and the federal compromise which seemed essential to enduring nationhood is once again in jeopardy.

There is disillusionment with the older parties, whose lack of distinguishing principles has probably augmented political instability; and in a period of prosperity, an acute dissatisfaction with the party in power is almost unique in Canadian history. On the other hand, the ideal of a common nationhood has not lost meaning for most Canadians.

Roloff Beny's evocation of the lonely expanses of Canada. ▶

National association on a transcontinental scale is, in their view, too precious a heritage to be whittled away in the interest of local rights and privileges. Although the idea of a distinct national identity may be a myth, they pray for a leadership possessing sufficient vision and inspiration to make their country's government effective at home and acceptable abroad. Mutual understanding between race and region is still far away, but an *entente cordiale* is not beyond the reach of men of imagination capable of rising to the level of events.

Unhappily for the French Canadian, the risk of engaging in national rather than provincial politics has always been high; to press the cause of national unity is to run the chance of being discredited by one's kinsfolk, as Laurier realized when he returned to his own people on the Conscription issue in 1917. In such circumstances, there is every likelihood that the strains and tensions will persist. The historic compromises of Baldwin and Lafontaine, Macdonald and Cartier, Laurier and Mackenzie King may prove insufficient to bridge the gulf that has been scoured out by religion, language, distrust and passion.

To suggest that all will end well is tempting, but such an estimate may have no other basis than an author's instinctive and wholesome optimism. Progress is not a law of nature. On the other hand, calculations founded on Canada's past and present racial difficulties may become irrelevant in the light of more ominous considerations. On a vast continent which modern technology seems intent on ironing to one mass level, Canadians may find it preferable to stick together, even if they find the process exasperating and sometimes even painful.

A Short Bibliography

GENERAL HISTORIES

Brebner, J.B., *The Explorers of North America 1492–1806* (London, 1933; 2nd edition, 1955).

Brown, George W. (editor), *Canada* (United Nations Series; Cambridge and University of California, 1950).

—, *Dictionary of Canadian Biography*, vol. I: 1000–1700 (Toronto, 1965).

Burt, A.L., *A Short History of Canada for Americans* (Minneapolis, 1944).

Careless, J.M.S., *Canada: A Story of Challenge*, revised edition (Toronto, 1966).

Cook, Ramsay, with Saywell, J.T., and Ricker, J.C., *Canada: A Modern Study* (Toronto, 1964).

Creighton, D.G., *Dominion of the North. A History of Canada*, new edition (London and Toronto, 1958).

Easterbrook, W.T., and Aitken, H.G.J., *Canadian Economic History* (Toronto, 1956)

Graham, G.S., *Canada: A Short History* (London, 1950).

Lower, A.R.M., *Colony to Nation*, 3rd edition (Toronto, 1957).

Morton, W.L., *The Kingdom of Canada. A General History from Earliest Times* (Toronto, 1963).

NEW FRANCE

Bishop, Morris, *Champlain: The Life of Fortitude* (New York, 1948).

Chapais, Thomas, *The Great Intendant, a Chronicle of Jean Talon in Canada, 1665–1672* (Toronto, 1921).

Eccles, W.J., *Frontenac: The Courtier Governor* (Toronto, 1959).

—, *Canada under Louis XIV 1663–1701* (Toronto, New York and London, 1964).

Frégault, Guy, *La Civilisation de la Nouvelle-France* (Montreal, 1944).

Harvey, D.C., *The French Régime in Prince Edward Island* (New Haven, 1926).

Hunt, G.T., *The Wars of the Iroquois* (Madison, Wisconsin, 1940).

Innis, H.A., *The Cod Fisheries*, revised edition (Toronto, 1954).

—, *The Fur Trade in Canada*, revised edition (Toronto, 1956).

—, *Select Documents in Canadian Economic History, 1497–1783* (Toronto, 1929).

Jenness, D., *The Indians of Canada* (Ottawa, 1932).

Lanctot, Gustave, *A History of Canada*, vol. I: *From its Origins to the Royal Régime, 1663*; vol. II: *From the Royal Régime to the Treaty of Utrecht, 1663–1713*; vol. III: *From the Treaty of Utrecht to the Treaty of Paris, 1713–1763* (Toronto and London, 1963, 1964 and 1965).

Long, M.H., *A History of the Canadian People*, vol. I: *New France* (Toronto, 1942).

MacKay, Douglas, *The Honourable Company. A History of the Hudson's Bay Company*, revised to 1949 (Toronto, 1949).

Munro, W.B., *The Seigniorial System in Canada* (Cambridge, Mass., 1907).

Parkman, Francis, *France and England in North America* (9 vols., various publishers and dates).

—, *Montcalm and Wolfe*, with a Foreword by Esmond Wright, Frontier Library (London, 1964).

Peckham, Howard H., *The Colonial Wars 1689–1762* (Chicago and London, 1964).

Rioux, Marcel, and Martin, Yves (editors), *French-Canadian Society* (Toronto, 1964).

THE BRITISH COLONIES BEFORE CONFEDERATION

Burt, A.L., *The Old Province of Quebec* (Minneapolis, 1933).

Careless, J.M.S., *Brown of the Globe*, vol. I: 1818–1859; vol. II: 1860–1880 (Toronto, 1959 and 1963).

Coupland, Reginald, *The Durham Report, an Abridged Version with an Introduction and Notes* (Oxford, 1945).

Cowan, Helen I., *British Emigration to British North America: The First Hundred Years* (Toronto, 1961).

Craig, G.M., *Upper Canada. The Formative Years, 1784–1841* (Toronto, 1963).

Creighton, D.G., *The (Commercial) Empire of the St Lawrence, 1760–1850* (Toronto, 1956).

Galbraith, John S., *The Hudson's Bay Company as an Imperial Factor, 1821–1869* (Berekeley and Los Angeles, 1957).

Graham, Gerald S., *Sea Power and British North America, 1783–1820* (Cambridge, Mass., 1941).

Hansen, M.L., and Brebner, J.B., *The Mingling of the Canadian and American Peoples* (Yale and Oxford, 1940).

Havighurst, Walter, *The Long Ships Passing. The Story of the Great Lakes* (New York, 1943).

Hitsman, J.M., *The Incredible War of 1812: A Military History* (Toronto, 1965).

Kerr, D.G.G., *Sir Edmund Head, a Scholarly Governor* (Toronto, 1954).

Kilbourn, William, *The Firebrand, William Lyon Mackenzie and the Rebellion in Upper Canada* (Toronto, 1956).

MacKay, R.A. (editor), *Newfoundland, Economic, Diplomatic and Strategic Studies* (Toronto and London, 1946).

Manning, Helen Taft, *The Revolt of French Canada, 1800–1835; a chapter of the history of the British Commonwealth* (London, 1962).

Martin, Chester, *Empire and Commonwealth* (Toronto and London, 1929).

Morison, J.L., *The Eighth Earl of Elgin* (London, 1928).

Morton, A.S., *A History of the Canadian West to 1870–1* (London, n.d.).

Neatby, Hilda M., *The Administration of Justice under the Quebec Act* (Minneapolis, 1937).

New, Chester, *Lord Durham* (London, 1929).

Rich, E.E., *History of the Hudson's Bay Company, 1670–1870*, 2 vols. (London, 1958 and 1959).

Stacey, C.P., *The Undefended Border: The Myth and the Reality*, No. 1, Canadian Historical Association, Historical Booklets (Ottawa, 1953).

Stanley, G.F.G., *Canada's Soldiers*, revised edition (Toronto, 1960).

Wade, Mason, *The French Canadians, 1760–1945* (Toronto, 1955).

Warner, D.F., *The Idea of Continental Union* (Louisville, 1960).

Whitelaw, W.M., *The Maritimes and Canada before Confederation* (Toronto, 1934).

Wilson, George E., *The Life of Robert Baldwin. A Study in the Struggle for Responsible Government* (Toronto, 1933).

Winks, R.W., *Canada and the United States: The Civil War Years* (Baltimore, 1960).

THE NATION

Cook, Ramsay, *Canada and the French-Canadian Question* (Toronto, 1966).

Creighton, D.G., *The Road to Confederation. The Emergence of Canada: 1863–1867* (Toronto, 1964).

—, *John A. Macdonald*, 2 vols. (Toronto and London, 1952 and 1955).

Dafoe, J.W., *Clifford Sifton in Relation to his Times* (Toronto, 1931).

—, *Laurier. A Study in Canadian Politics* (Toronto, 1922).

Dawson, C.A. (editor), *The New North-West* (Toronto, 1947).

Dawson, R.M., *William Lyon Mackenzie King: A Political Biography, 1874–1923* (Toronto, 1959).

—, *The Government of Canada* (Toronto, 1947).

Eayrs, James, *The Art of the Possible: Government and Foreign Policy in Canada* (Toronto, 1961).

—, *In Defence of Canada. From the Great War to the Great Depression* (Toronto, 1965).

Farr, D.M.L., *The Colonial Office and Canada, 1867–1887* (Toronto, 1955).

Ferns, H.S., and Ostry, B., *The Age of Mackenzie King: The Rise of the Leader* (London, 1956).

Gilbert, Heather, *Awaking Continent, The Life of Lord Mount Stephen*, vol. I: *1829–91* (Aberdeen, 1965).

Glazebrooke, G.P. de T., *A History of Transportation in Canada* (Toronto, 1938).

Graham, Roger, *Arthur Meighen*, vol. I: *The Door of Opportunity*; vol. II: *And Fortune Fled*; vol. III: *No Surrender* (Toronto, 1960, 1963 and 1965).

Grant, G.P., *Lament for a Nation. The Defeat of Canadian Nationalism* (Toronto, 1965).

Hedges, J.B., *Building the Canadian West, the Land and Colonization Policies of The Canadian Pacific Railway* (New York, 1939).

Irving, J.A., *The Philosophy of Social Credit* (Toronto, 1959).

Lower, A.R.M., *Canadians in the Making* (Toronto, 1958).

Lysenko, Vera, *Men in Sheepskin Coats: A Study in Assimilation* (Toronto, 1947).

MacNutt, W.S., *The Atlantic Provinces. The Emergence of Colonial Society 1812–1857* (Toronto, 1965).

Moir, J.S., *Church and State in Canada West* (Toronto, 1959).

Morton, W.L., *The Progressive Party in Canada* (Toronto, 1950).

—, *The Critical Years: The Union of British North America, 1857–1873* (Toronto, 1964).

Neatby, H.B., *William Lyon Mackenzie King, 1924–1932. The Lonely Heights* (Toronto, 1963).

Parker, J., *Newfoundland, 10th Province of Canada* (London, 1950).

Penlington, Norman, *Canada and Imperialism, 1896–1899* (Toronto, 1965).

Pickersgill, J.W., *The Mackenzie King Record.* Vol. I: *1939–1944* (Toronto, 1960).

Quinn, Herbert F., *The Union Nationale. A Study in Quebec Nationalism* (Toronto, 1963).

Sharp, Paul F., *Whoop-Up Country: The Canadian-American West, 1865–1885* (Toronto, 1956).

Stanley, G.F.G., *The Birth of Western Canada. A History of the Riel Rebellions* (new edition, Toronto, 1960).

Skelton, O.D., *The Life and Letters of Sir Wilfrid Laurier*, 2 vols. (Toronto, 1921).

Stevens, G.R., *Canadian National Railways.* Vol. I: *Sixty Years of Trial and Error (1836–1896)*; vol. II: *Towards the Inevitable (1896–1922)* (Toronto, 1960 and 1962).

Thomas, L.H., *The Struggle for Responsible Government in the North-West Territories, 1870–1897* (Toronto, 1956).

Waite, P.B., *The Life and Times of Confederation, 1864–1867* (Toronto, 1961).

Wheare, K.C., *The Statute of Westminster and Dominion Status*, 5th edition (London, 1953).

THE ARTS

Bissell, C.T. (editor), *Our Living Tradition. Seven Canadians* (Toronto, 1957).

Brown, E.K., *On Canadian Poetry*, 2nd edition (Toronto, 1945).

Buchanan, D.W., *The Growth of Canadian Painting* (London, 1950).

Clark, S.D., *The Social Development of Canada* (Toronto, 1942).

McDougall, Robert L. (editor), *Our Living Tradition*, Second and Third Series (Toronto, 1959).

— (editor), *Our Living Tradition*, Fourth Series (Toronto, 1962).

A Short Bibliography

Massey, Vincent, *On Being Canadian* (London, 1948).

—, (Chairman) *Report of the Royal Commission on National Development in the Arts, Letters and Sciences, 1949–1951* (Ottawa, 1951).

Pacey, Desmond, *Creative Writing in Canada. A Short History of English-Canadian Literature*, revised edition (Toronto, 1961).

Park, Julian (editor), *The Culture of Contemporary Canada*, containing an essay by Professor Roy Daniells, 'Poetry and the Novel' (Ithaca, New York, 1957).

Ross, M. M. (editor), *Our Sense of Identity. A Book of Canadian Essays* (Toronto, 1944).

— (editor), *The Arts in Canada: a stock-taking at Mid-century* (London, 1959).

Smith, A. J. M. (editor), *The Book of Canadian Poetry, a Critical and Historical Anthology* (Chicago, 1943).

Viatte, A., *L'Histoire littéraire de l'Amérique Français des origines à 1950* (Quebec, 1954).

List of Illustrations